MY
MOM
IS MY
HERO

EDITED BY
SUSAN REYNOLDS

MY MOM IS MY HERO

Tributes to the Women Who Gave Us
Life, Love, and Clean Laundry

adamsmedia

AVON, MASSACHUSETTS

Published by
Adams Media, a division of F+W Media, Inc.
57 Littlefield Street, Avon, MA 02322. U.S.A.
www.adamsmedia.com

ISBN 10: 1-59869-791-9
ISBN 13: 978-1-59869-791-9

Printed in the United States of America.

J I H G F E D C B A

Library of Congress Cataloging-in-Publication Data
is available from the publisher.

This publication is designed to provide accurate and authoritative information
with regard to the subject matter covered. It is sold with the understanding that
the publisher is not engaged in rendering legal, accounting, or other professional advice. If legal advice or other expert assistance is required, the services of
a competent professional person should be sought.

—From a *Declaration of Principles* jointly adopted by a Committee of the
American Bar Association and a Committee of Publishers and Associations

Many of the designations used by manufacturers and sellers to distinguish their
product are claimed as trademarks. Where those designations appear in this
book and Adams Media was aware of a trademark claim, the designations have
been printed with initial capital letters.

This book is available at quantity discounts for bulk purchases.
For information, please call 1-800-289-0963.

*I dedicate this anthology to the mothers
who most shaped my life:*
my mother, Grace Sue Reynolds;
my maternal grandmother, Irma Pillow Pennington;
my paternal grandmother, Eunice Partridge Reynolds;
and my maternal great-grandmother, Cordelia Scott Pillow.
Each—in her own way—was an amazingly strong woman.

I also dedicate this to all mothers who lovingly guide their
children through the maze.

Contents

Acknowledgments

I offer gratitude to the mothers in my family, all of whom have inspired me throughout my life, in particular: my sister Rozanne Reynolds; my sisters-in-law Karen Reynolds and Suryea Reynolds; and my nieces Michele Kaczmarek Correll, Amy Reynolds, and Angela Reynolds. I would also like to honor Jan Berry Kadrie, Faye Lyle, Virginia Shafer, and Norma Jaichima all of whom shared their wisdom and dispensed needed affection while "mothering" me during difficult times.

At Adams Media, I'd like to thank Paula Munier for her vision and her invaluable editorial direction, project manager Brendan O'Neill for his tireless efforts to do the best editing possible, editorial assistant Sara Stock for her dedicated assistance, and everyone else involved at Adams from production to promotion for their enthusiasm for this series. Also, I would like to offer a special thanks to *Cup of Comfort®* editor Colleen Sell for offering her mailing list and ideas about where to find writers with meaningful stories to tell.

I sincerely thank the contributors who so generously shared their mother stories for all of us to enjoy! Thank you for honoring your unique and marvelous mothers, grandmothers, and mother figures. The book will live as a testament to them, and their stories will touch our readers' lives.

And finally, as always, I will be eternally grateful to my beloved children, Brooke Sandon Aved and Brett Allen Aved, who continue to enrich my life in ways they will only fully understand when they become parents.

Introduction

As the brilliant mythologist Joseph Campbell once taught, no one is more heroic than a mother. After all, choosing to give birth provides the ultimate journey, one that can be both perilous and exhilarating, one that can end in the ultimate tragedy of death or the ultimate reward of new life. Even when a mother navigates pregnancy and delivery successfully, no other life experience compares to the never-ending adventure of motherhood. From the moment we cross the threshold, we rely on our mothers' wellsprings of nourishment and nurturance to fulfill our most basic physical and emotional needs. Mothers hold us, feed us, burp us, change us, bath us, comfort us, protect us, clothe us, teach us, and guide us. Without our mothers, we are lost.

The fifty stories contained in this volume offer fascinating portraits of the mother, grandmother, aunt, or mother figure who greatly affected the author's life. The stories are alternately poignant, sweet, humorous, heartbreaking, and heartwarming. The women captured are uniquely impressive, inspirational, colorful, funny, quirky, outrageous, determined, brave, inventive, imaginative, generous, kind, forgiving, and—above all—memorable.

There's something for every reader and something from a breadth of writers—from young voices to wizened voices. One young writer compares his mother to a superhero, allotting her laser-like perceptions and a lethal ray. Another young woman writes about her struggles with depression and a teenage pregnancy, depicting the strength and forbearance her mother showed during her darkest days. Another young man spends an entire weekend attempting to ditch his bothersome mother at a sports conference, only to rediscover the mysterious bond that he can only assume is love.

Two writers—one male, one female—offer tautly and expertly written stories about attempted molestations and how their mothers became fierce tigresses unleashing and exerting their ultimate mother instincts.

We have a number of war stories, some dating back to World War I, more to World War II. Harrowing tales of survival on both sides of the fight depict mothers whose actions saved their children from certain death. From encampments to bomb shelters to late night escapes, each tale reminds us the vital role mothers play in times of unimaginable duress. One story recounts the incredible bravery of a young woman traveling from Pinsk to Moscow in the winter of 1919 so she can study medicine and become one of the first female doctors in Moscow. She displays a century of courage that so inspired her daughter she literally followed in her mother's footsteps.

Because we have a number of writers grateful to their mothers for inspiring them at an early age, we have several stories about mothers who were gifted storytellers—so good you want to curl up at their feet to listen. One writer's mother absconded bits and pieces of broken wooden cartons to build him a writing desk so he would dare to follow his dream rather than spend his life picking cotton in the scorching Oklahoma fields. Several writers offer vivid portraits of mothers who loved literature so well they introduced their lucky children to its particular brand of magic.

And we have humor—lots of humor! From the mother who smacks a peeping Tom off his ladder to the mother who returns half-eaten Thanksgiving turkeys to the toughened rancher who refuses to move a dead horse off her property, we have stories that will delight and enthrall.

I absolutely fell in love with these writers, these stories, and these mothers (grandmothers, aunts, and mother figures), and I know you will too—as will the mother, grandmother, aunt, or mother figure you would like to honor by presenting her this collection of stories. This book serves as a testament to the art of mothering, and it will entertain any reader. So curl up and get ready to meet some unforgettable women.

The Care Package Queen

KATHRYN GODSIFF

The white cardboard box sat on the table, a slightly scruffy centerpiece, a treasure box of longed-for treats, a product of loving hands. My three young sons circled like sharks, waiting for my husband to come in from his day's work on our New Zealand sheep and cattle farm. A pot of tea brewed nearby, the scissors were out to cut the tape, and the customs form, giving away the secrets of the box, had been torn off unread. When we heard the clump of work boots in the washhouse, the boys mobbed their father, dragging him into the kitchen. Now we could finally see what my mom, the care package queen, had sent us this time.

This tradition of sending little pieces of home to those far away must be as old as motherhood. My mom started the summer of my junior year at high school while I worked at a youth camp for a month. Every week when the mail arrived, there would be a box addressed to me. Nobody got care packages every week, the office lady told me. Instead of squirming with embarrassment at that news, I felt honored by my mother. And I basked in the light of popularity for as long as it took to devour the edible portions of the package. My mother was the best cookie baker in a three-state region, at least in our family's opinion. She stayed true to her reputation with each box. Chocolate chip oatmeal crispies, snickerdoodles, gingersnaps, brownies, and my favorite, date cookies, satisfied teenage sweet tooths.

My mom also included news from home. She told me what the cat and dog had done, what she had fixed for dinner for my brother and dad, where she'd gone exploring that week. (She was a teacher enjoying her summer vacation.) She cut out sections of the Sunday comics that I'd like. She sent a T-shirt she'd bought on sale. The boxes and letters were her way of keeping a line glowing between us during my first time away from home.

I'm not sure where my mom acquired this knack for speaking her love without words. Perhaps it was from her taciturn grandmother, who raised my mom in a small Idaho mining town. She grew up understanding that the blank spaces between words can be filled with small and special things.

Mom's care package commitment was put to the test when I became an exchange student to New Zealand my junior year at college. Sending things airmail was expensive, so boxes arrived by ship. The journey took six weeks, and not many cookies retain their freshness for that long. She got creative with other items. Graham crackers, M&M's, chocolate chips, gummy bears, magazines, film for my camera, undies, sweaters, new contact lenses, and note cards all found their way to the South Island. It was comfort stuff, not available there and somehow Mom knew just when it was needed. She sent five boxes that year.

My time in New Zealand did more than hone my mother's care packaging skills. I'd also met my future husband, a fourth generation sheep and cattle farmer. We married in the United States and managed an Oregon sheep farm for nearly a year, so Mom got a break from sending boxes. She delivered the goodies in person. But inevitably we headed back to New Zealand to continue our farming life and raise a family.

For eighteen years, my mom sent us care packages from her home in the Pacific Northwest. When I was expecting our first baby, she organized a baby shower. She gathered a group of my dearest friends, set up a tape recorder and had a camera ready. The girls brought the presents unwrapped, and then they showed them around to each other. After each gift was admired, it was wrapped and packed into a box. Then the felt pens came out, and the girls decorated the box. When all was completed, they had tea and cake, took more pictures, and clicked off the tape recorder and put the cassette in. As soon as the photos were developed, my mom tucked them into the box and sent it off. This most precious care package arrived a few weeks after the birth of our son; it was the only baby shower I had.

Three or four times a year we'd circle the table, anticipating opening the boxes. They had a particular smell, a nice one accumulated despite the long voyage. The scent represented something special to our boys. When I brought my youngest to Washington State for a visit, the first thing he said when he walked into my parents' home was, "It smells like America." He recognized the aroma of love that surrounded us when we'd open a box from my mom.

She learned to tell by lifting the boxes if they were within weight range. She knew her local postal workers by name. The boxes came decorated with happy sayings like "Hug a sheep today" or "Happy Birthday" or "Hope you like the loot." In all those years, we never had to pay duty on any of her gifts. I suspect the customs inspectors looked forward to the boxes as much as we did.

My mom had a shelf in her home set aside for our goodies. She'd see something she thought we would like, and it would go into the stash until there was enough to fill a box. She sent children's books set in the West and would include a tape of her reading the book. Through her care packages, my sons learned their grandmother's voice. She was able to visit us just five times in those eighteen years, so most of her grandmothering was done long-distance. We spoke by phone once a month, wrote letters, and grew closer.

The greatest gift my mother sent in all those boxes was her unconditional love. It made my homesickness bearable, keeping "home" alive and letting our boys know they have a special dual heritage. It kept us all—my husband, our sons, and me—bound to family so far away. Through her choice of books and games, our boys learned about American history and geography. They also got cool toys and clothes.

We now live in the United States, and my mom doesn't have to send packages nearly 10,000 miles. She still keeps an eye out for things we'd like, little stuff that lets us know she's glad we're close by. The best care package these days is her car; it stops outside our house and we circle around it, waiting to open it up and hug the treasure inside.

KATHRYN GODSIFF lives in Sisters, Oregon, where she and her husband manage a small ranch. She writes for the local newspaper and a regional equestrian magazine. Her essays have appeared in *Chick Ink: 40 Stories of Tattoos—and the Women Who Wear Them* and *A Cup of Comfort® for Dog Lovers*.

Fury

LAURA PRITCHETT

When Fury finally dies, he picks a back pasture on my parents' Colorado ranch to rest his old horse body. The neighbor across the fence calls to tell my mother this: There's now a dead horse, which he can see from his kitchen window. My mother doesn't like this new neighbor. "He's new, obnoxious, and, doesn't know a darn thing about how to love these mountains." Clearly, she is not sympathetic.

He asks what she plans on doing with the horse. She says, in her characteristic pleasant-but-serious ranch woman voice, that she'll let the horse be. Here is a woman who has protected her ranch with more spunk and energy than a mountain lion. She's saved it from developers, bike trails, power lines, and a nearby city's huge water pipes. She's balanced the books, forbidden hunting, and raised everything from peacocks to donkeys. She watched the birth of three Arab horses, which she later trained and rode all over these mountains. She's lugged newborn calves into our kitchen in the middle of winter to resuscitate and save them, she's helped many a mama cow deliver a turned or heavy baby, and she's kept company with bears and chased away the rattlesnakes. She's raised nine children to be as honest, true, and tough as she is herself. So a new, grumpy, city slicker neighbor is not something she fears.

That's why, when the neighbor demands that she move the carcass, she simply says she will not.

He says she will.

She says she will not.

He says she will.

She tells him he can move it himself. They hang up on each other.

He calls again; this time they are calmer. She tries hard to explain. She tells him the rendering truck can't get to the horse, because the horse chose to die in a pasture past the two irrigation canals, and the bridges are rickety and old. She tells him the carcass can't be buried, either, because a backhoe can't get back there, and the ground is sheer rock underneath the topsoil.

He says, "Something has got to be done. The smell and the rotting, bloating carcass cannot remain!"

After a pause, she says, "Look, we don't owe you a view. Plus, looking at a dead horse is better than having to look at your house."

He asks, "Are you comparing my beautiful house to a dead horse?"

"No," she says, "Yours is far worse. The horse will be gone in a few weeks, but your house is up there ruining the view forever."

He hangs up on her.

The fight escalates. The neighbor calls the Health Department, but the officials there tell him that a decaying horse on a rancher's own property does not constitute a health hazard. The neighbor writes a letter to my mother, accusing her of various atrocities. She smiles and ignores him. Neighbors watch, amused, and side with my mother.

Within a few weeks, there isn't a trace left of Fury. Some animals chewed on him, but mostly maggots worked on him until the only thing left was the skull, which my brother salvaged sometime during the decaying process. This, he plopped into my mother's garden, where it rests with deer antlers, cow skulls, fox jaws, an old signal from a long-deserted railroad track, the tail of a (naturally deceased) fox hanging from a stick, and a red marble tombstone for an old beloved dog.

This spring, my mother will garden around the skull of Fury, and I suppose the vegetables she brings to my house will have flourished around the bones of our old horse. And probably we will chuckle over the fact that Fury, so calm in life, finally lived up to his name in the end.

I will hug her, completely enamored. How can I not love a woman who has such a fierce, protective, life-nurturing fury?

LAURA PRITCHETT is the author of a novel *Sky Bridge* (winner of the WILLA Literary Award) and a collection of short stories, *Hell's Bottom, Colorado* (winner of the PEN USA Award). Pritchett is also co-editor of three books: *Home Land*, *The Pulse of the River*, and *Going Green: True Tales from Gleaners, Scavengers, and Dumpster Divers*. Pritchett's work has also appeared in numerous magazines and several books, including *Comeback Wolves* and *Social Issues Firsthand: The Environment*.

The Writing Desk

CHARLES W. SASSER

I see her still beneath the hard Oklahoma sun. Her slatted bonnet faded pale like the November sky, her back bent into the ten-foot "pick-sack" she dragged down endless cotton rows, calloused fingers plucking fiber from bolls with amazing speed. Three cents a pound, three dollars a hundred paid cash upon weigh-in at the scales. Mom earned four dollars on a good day. I was eight or so; I picked a hundred and made three dollars. Joe was two years younger; he picked fifty or sixty pounds from the time the dew burned off in the morning until the "cotton truck" loaded up at sunset to deliver us home.

Home was never much. Once, we occupied a dirt-floored former chicken house. Another time we lived in a barn next to a cotton field. We paid ten dollars a year to rent an upscale three-room shack with a tin roof and no interior walls or insulation—no electricity or plumbing—with a wood-burning cane heater, kerosene lamps, and a kerosene stove over which Mom cooked supper at the end of a long day in the fields.

My mother had to quit school after the eighth grade and had been doing hard labor all her life. My stepdad dropped out of the first grade and could neither read nor write. He was one of those small-headed men with big hands whose ignorance and suspicion had worn his brain down to a nubbin. Mom probably married him because she thought a poor girl from the hills—kicked out on her own when she was sixteen because she was pregnant out of wedlock with me and then had another fatherless son by the time she was eighteen—couldn't do any better. My stepdad believed we were born to be poor, and so we were, so *down-and-dirty* poor that generic poverty felt like a step up.

One of the biggest thrills in my childhood came when my Aunt Ellen gave me a box of books. Until then, the only books in our house were Sears, Roebuck, and Co. catalogs, and those only because they proved useful in the outhouse. With Mom's help, I employed the gifted books to teach myself to read.

"You're real smart, smarter 'n the rest of us," Mom would say, her tired face lighting up in a rare show of enthusiasm. "You get yourself a good education, son, and you can do things I ain't never had courage to dream about."

Every time my stepdad caught me reading, he protested vigorously. "Mossie, that boy done got his G**d*** nose stuck in a book again. You ought not to give him no ideas; he ain't never gonna be worth a damn."

My grandfather had beaten my mother regularly, with well ropes, harness check-lines, tree limbs, belts, and even chains. My stepdad never beat her, but he bullied her so religiously she usually had the good sense to clam up.

I, on the other hand, often chose open defiance. "Reading ain't hurting nobody," I would reply, dodging his fist.

"What good's it ever done me or anybody else? You got to learn to work, not read."

Despite his blustering, I kept my nose in any books I could get my hands on. At every opportunity, I'd sneak off into the woods to read. Occasionally, Mom hoarded a few cents, and when she went to town and had enough, she'd buy me a book, sneak it home, and slip it to me when he wasn't looking. In those days, a quarter or thirty-five cents for a paperback, particularly when we desperately needed shoes and cornmeal, amounted to a minor fortune.

"Don't say nothing to your dad," Mom cautioned, putting her scarred hands to her lips in a shushing motion. "One of these days, son, you *are* gonna be somebody I can be proud of. You ain't gonna slave in cotton fields like I done."

"I want to be a writer like Ernest Hemingway," I said, gleefully. "I'll go on adventures . . . and then write about them."

When I acted this way, my stepdad suggested I might be legitimately loony. Everyone laughed at the notion that a ragged hillbilly kid born and raised in a cotton field might grow up to be a writer, or that he would ever be worth a damn.

Everyone laughed, except Mom. "Don't you *never* listen to them," she said. "They poke fun at you 'cause they never done nothing themselves, and they don't have the smarts you do."

When Mom discovered a couple of discarded packing crates, she rounded up some used one-by-eight lumber, and then spent several Sundays—when we weren't in the field—hammering and sawing behind our shack. A smile lit up her worn, lined face when she finished. She had fashioned a writing desk—for me!

Together we moved it into the kitchen against a wall. She brought me a kerosene lamp, an old fountain pen, a well of ink she scrounged up somewhere, and a stack of used paper that was blank on only one side. I found a wooden box and used it as a makeshift shelf to house my books. I had my own desk . . . and my own library!

"You're giving that kid fancy ideas," my stepdad scoffed.

Mom must have held firm against him, for that wonderful desk found its way to whatever shanty or shack we lived in from then on. I rose before daylight every morning, built a fire in the wood burner, lit my lamp, sat down at my desk, imagined a vast and marvelous new world, and then wrote down everything that sprang to my mind.

By the time I was ten, I had written hundreds of short stories and a complete novel entitled *Devil Mountain*. Nothing proved publishable, but it didn't matter. Someday they would. Cotton fields soon lost their menace. I no longer felt doomed to them. Mom had opened a secret door through which escape became possible.

One afternoon, as the cotton truck was delivering field hands home after a day's work, I overheard a snippet of conversation that sent my heart suddenly soaring. I had sunk onto my folded pick-sack next to the tailgate of the tarp-covered truck. My little brother Joe had scooted over to cozy up and soon dozed on my shoulder. Mom had crowded onto one of the wooden benches and removed her bonnet. As we rolled along, watching the sun set in a burst of crimson and violet that spread breathtaking color all the way across the Arkansas River bottoms, she and another picker chatted about the weather, how much cotton they had weighed in today . . . and, finally, their kids.

"Now you take my son Charles," Mom said, puffing up. "He ain't gonna be pickin' cotton the rest of his life. My Charles, he's a *writer.*"

CHARLES W. SASSER has been a full-time freelance writer for twenty-nine years. He has published more than fifty books and 3,000 magazine articles and short stories. View news of his work on *www.charlessasser.com*.

Killing Cows

S. AARON SPRIGGS

Texas summer winds were pelting dust against the window-panes when she noticed movement through the parted curtains and spotted a pair of pale eyes peering through the window. Without hesitation, my young mother thrust her hand straight through the glass and smack into the face of a peeping Tom. Although petite—five foot, four inches and no rounder than a willow branch—my mom hit the voyeur so hard she knocked him off his ladder and smack on his butt in the yard.

My father dashed outside with his gun, but the man had disappeared, abandoning the ladder in his wake. Mom called the local sheriff, who came out right away and was quite sympathetic. A peeping Tom had reportedly been casing the area for a while, but no one had been able to catch him. "If he happens to show up again, and I have to come out here again, and you happened to have nicked the pervert, Mr. Spriggs—or Mrs. Spriggs," the sheriff said, nodding in deference to my mom's assertive action, "just make sure the body is in the house by the time I arrive."

The next day, my dad and a neighbor canvassed the area, including the fields nearby. When they found a stash of ladders chained together, Dad cut the chain and distributed the ladders amongst the neighbors. For as long as my parents lived in that Texas house, no more peeping Toms were ever sighted in the area. And they still have that ladder.

But that's not the only story we tell about my mother, and it's not how she ended up with a monstrous scar on her arm. When it came to that peeping Tom, Mom punched so straight she didn't even cut her hands or her arm on the window. I think of that story every time I see her scar, but my little dynamo of a mom already had the scar by the time she took out the peeping Tom.

Shortly before moving to Texas, my parents—Regina and Bob—a young, energetic couple, were driving late at night with me strapped into the backseat of their sea-foam green, '67 Chevy, two-door hardtop. It was pitch black in the middle of Nowhere, South Dakota, and the moon was miniscule.

Unexpectedly, a pair of eyes materialized right in front of them, floating in the headlights. Just before the impact, they both realized a black cow had turned its head at the precise moment their lights shined on it. My father didn't even have time to hit the brakes and did the only thing he could—he jerked the wheel. They missed the black cow, but they plowed into the herd of cows that had been following the first cow across the road. A mighty thud followed and a series of smaller thuds until the car came to a jerking stop.

The second the impacts halted, Mom instantaneously flipped around to retrieve me from the back seat. Shattered window glass covered every surface in the car, including me. When she thrust her arm back and waggled it across the seat to find my seat belt, a shard scrapped the length of her arm, creating what the family later came to call her "badge of honor" mentioned in reference, of course, to "the night mom and dad killed the cows."

As soon as my mother had me in her grasp, my parents exited the car. Moments later, another car crashed into my parent's car. The driver was surely blinded by the night, but he also proved to be inebriated, so while Dad helped the staggering driver escape his vehicle, Mom and I struck out for the closest house. Carrying me, she thrust her tiny legs as fast as they could go through the thick roadside weeds, through a pasture, about 200 yards to the only house in sight. By the time we arrived, blood had soaked her clothing to the point she was dripping wet.

Frightened by the sight, the rancher kept her on the porch, failing to quiet the German Shepard who jumped and barked and squawked. "If you don't call that dog off," Mom said, "I'll kick his teeth in." The rancher opened the door and let Mom use his telephone to call for help. Eventually, he admitted that he let his cows roam free in the night, and he accepted the fact that they had been a public nuisance. But he was too stunned and inept to do anything, so Mom snatched up his telephone and dialed the hospital herself, dripping blood on the rancher's floor while he sat in a corner fretting about how to deal with his dead cows.

So that's how my brave, fierce Mom got the monstrous scar that brands her arm. Now I have plenty of my own scars, but none as large as Mom's. I have my own ladder, but I didn't punch out a pervert to get it. I've eaten plenty of hamburgers, but I've never butchered my own cow. Mom sets a mean standard.

S. AARON SPRIGGS is an arachnologist/entomologist at the Denver Museum of Nature & Science. When not idolizing his mom, he plays trumpet and theremin and writes fiction, poetry, and road-kill Haiku. He felt compelled to write this story, despite years of harassment from his mom for wearing his trademark Mohawk and repeatedly attending Burning Man, an annual art event and temporary community based on radical self-expression and self-reliance in the Black Rock Desert of Nevada.

A Certain Kind of Magic

WENDY LYNN CLARK

I am a child of fantasy, of one rings and knights errant, and I know I got this from my mother. She's read all the Harry Potter books. Sometimes I catch her late at night, quietly turning the pages, a chocolate wrapper crumpled into the folds of the couch. She does this surreptitiously, because she's the healthy-eater-early-riser in our family; my father is the late-show pretzel junkie. She likes Harry Potter, I think, because she recognizes the importance of spells. Ordinary words, like magic words, can wield extraordinary power at the right time.

When I was tall enough for nail polish but still small enough to fit under her elbow, we attended a family holiday party. Good cheer overflowed the Dixie cups and goblets of the guests. I wore a new velveteen dress, sucked on little squares of maple penuche that we only ate at Christmas, and avoided a certain uncle who lived far away. We saw each other rarely. Something about him seemed slightly off, such that if you tilted your head and listened in a certain way, you could almost hear it.

He stuffed his weight into checkered shirts and squinted behind thick glasses. Sparse hairs flopped like fat worms across his baldpate. In his childhood, his father had often beaten him until he screamed, and at some point, he got broken. Being broken wasn't considered so much of a crime then, if it happened within the family.

As we were leaving this party, while everyone hugged and clustered around the front door, I snuck into the living room for a final square of candy. Only my uncle remained on the afghan-covered davenport. Because he seemed lonely, I swallowed the penuche and smiled.

"Aren't you going to say goodbye?" he asked. His mouth moved in a smile that didn't meet the rest of his face.

I hesitated. The call of magic was then still strong, and I knew of demons, but thought they only lurked in the undersides of forests. I waved.

"That's all I get?" he asked. "No hug?"

I did not want to put my arms around him, not even in a living room a few feet from all my nearest relatives laughing and talking, but women's self-defense doesn't teach it's okay to say no until college. I walked forward and stiffly put my arms out to hug his shoulders. It was the part I thought I could reach all the way around.

He grabbed me around the waist and lifted me on his lap, twisted so I faced outward. At nine, I was nearly too old for my dad's lap at our bedtime story hour. I sat rigidly, my velveteen dress crushed up against this stranger's chest, his hands locked over me.

"I've got you," he said in my ear. "Whatcha going to do now?"

I squirmed. He released his grip just long enough for me to lean forward. As I started to push myself off, he pulled me back again like a seatbelt jerked too hard.

"Oh!" he cried, laughing. "I gotcha!"

This happened three times. Each time I saw and felt freedom, and each time he snatched it away from me. Somehow, we ended up horizontal on the couch. I struggled silently, for I was old enough to know better than to make a scene. The cut of helplessness eroded my determination, and he laughed too loudly in my ear. My family, so few feet away, didn't hear.

There is a danger to those who live in fantasy. Tricked into believing all battles must be epic, they make paper dragons and slay them in magnificent conflagrations, while the true dragons, of flesh and skin, creep dangerously close. It's the simple moments when the real battles are fought, and nobody even notices.

My mother was suddenly standing right in front of us.

"Let her go," she said. Her voice carried over the hubbub, not with volume but with authority.

He loosened his arms. I scooted forward, and he snatched me back, laughing. "Who's going to make me?"

She stepped forward. Her eyes widened and her nostrils flared. "You are going to let go of her. And never touch her again."

He laughed as though she meant it as a joke. I sat rigidly, watching to see if I was about to get in trouble. Her gaze didn't waver.

His grin faltered. He opened his arms, and I scooted off. Following me up, he grabbed my mom and pinned her arms to her sides. "Now I've got you." He grinned with broken teeth.

She lifted her chin. "You will let go of me right now."

"Or else what?"

They froze like that, my mom tense and defiant, my uncle opening his mouth. I ran out to the quieted hall and into the arms of my dad. My mom emerged a moment later, cheeks flushed and hair mussed. My uncle did not follow her.

She kept me beside her as we pushed through relatives to the front door, ignoring their frowns and murmurs about overreaction. More than once she'd been the silent victim. In the crossover generation, raised by the ones who averted their eyes, she birthed me, the generation who face down demons wherever they appear, in forests or in family living rooms. She understood that the momentary silence of a group was more important than the permanent silence of the one, and her magic carried me away into the soft safety of the night.

***

WENDY LYNN CLARK travels the world befriending the good dragons and slaying the bad. Her favorite fantasies involve tropical beaches and drinks that come with little colored umbrellas.

Reader Extraordinaire

NANCY KELLY ALLEN

lick, clack, click, clack, click, clack, ding! Mom's fingers pounded the typewriter keys like a woodpecker hammering an oak tree. Following the last keystroke, she freed the paper from the roller, then fluttered her fingers in the air in dramatic fashion and blew on their tips. "These hot fingers need to cool down," she explained with a smile and a wink.

With cooled fingers, Mom lifted me into her lap. I squirmed, scooted, and got comfortable. She rolled a fresh sheet of white paper into the magical machine, and we were off on an adventure. She taught me how to punch the keys and type my name. We started with my first name and with practice, progressed to my middle and last names.

Mom, alone, made up the entire clerical staff of Dad's small mining company. Her corner office with a view was just that: a small corner in a small bedroom of our house. The view overlooked the steps leading down to the basement.

Mom proudly claimed the titles of wife, homemaker, cook, and others too numerous to mention, each of which claimed her time and energy. Through it all, she found spare moments each day to take me to her corner office and let me pound away on her typewriter.

With flourish, I wriggled my fingers in a limbering exercise I had seen my mother perform on a daily basis. I grabbed a sheet of paper and rolled it into the typewriter. As Mom swept the floors, made beds, and answered the phone on business calls, I pecked at the keys. My keystrokes were slow and random, more like a bingo player covering a card with chips, than a swift, on-target woodpecker. A bingo player eventually yells, "Bingo," and so did I as I finished the last line of my original tale.

Mom rushed in. "What did you type?" she asked, anxious to read my creation.

I fluttered my fingers in the air and blew on the tips to cool them down. "A story," I answered. I tugged at the paper to pull it out of the typewriter. "Read it to me."

Eemmmmmmm. Mom cleared her throat and looked down at our two dogs, Coalie and Skeeter. "Ladies and Gentlemen, our story today is *Two Dogs in a Race* written by a four-year-old author with an amazing talent. I'm afraid I can't reveal the name of the author because she would become so famous she would have to leave home and spend her days doing nothing but writing stories."

Before Mom could read the first line of my mumble-jumble writing, Skeeter barked.

"Hold your applause, please, until the reading is finished," Mom said.

Coalie joined in with a couple of barks of his own.

"My oh my, you are an excited audience. I promise, you won't be disappointed." Mom began reading with theatrical flair. "*Two Dogs in a Race* by Nancy. *Oops*! I revealed the name of the author." She clasped her hand over her mouth as though she had committed a major faux pas.

I giggled. Skeeter barked. Coalie chased his tail and yipped.

"I must remind the audience to hold your applause until *after* the reading," Mom announced with mock disdain.

I giggled again, but this time Coalie curled up on a rug to listen, and I grabbed Skeeter and lifted her onto my lap.

Mom "read" my story, as the title implied, about two dogs in a race.

Wow! I thought as I hung on to every word. I didn't realize I had written anything, much less a real story with real characters in a real adventure.

"Skeeter limped along holding up his front right paw," Mom embellished the story with intricate details as she continued reading. "Coalie tore off in the opposite direction when he saw the rabbit."

Skeeter and Coalie wagged their tails, as Mom read their names. I sat, still as the keys on the typewriter, as I listened, but my heart played thumpety-thump in my chest. I was astonished at my talent for creating stories, especially because I had not learned to write words, other than my name. The more Mom read of the story, the more amazed I became.

After Mom pronounced, "The end," she clapped her hands. A handclap or two was all the incentive Skeeter needed to leap out of my lap and yip with excitement. Coalie jumped up and ran in circles chasing his tail.

"Take a bow," Mom said to me with a wide-open smile. She bent at the waist and crossed one leg in front of the other to show me how. Her arms stretched out like wings. I followed her example and bowed to my audience. Skeeter and Coalie showed their appreciation with face licks and tail wags.

Later that evening, Mom whipped out my masterpiece and read it to Dad, Uncle Howard, and my brother, Ronald. Once again, I received thunderous applause, which I followed with a bow and a smile.

"That's pretty good writing for someone who has not learned to read," my brother said.

I wiggled my hot fingers in the air and blew on their tips. "It's the magic of a typewriter," I explained and really believed my explanation. Years later, of course, I realized the magic was in my mother, whose legacy lives on in my spirited writing.

NANCY KELLY ALLEN is a former teacher and librarian who now spends her days writing books for children. Two canine muses, Pippin Pooh and Harrietta Scattercat, provide creative incentives with face licks and tail wags. Sample Nancy's award-winning writing at *www.nancykellyallen.com*.

She Definitely Loves Me

JUDY GERLACH

Mom smiled and shook her head as she observed the way I stared at the metal lock box on the shelf. Even though I was only fourteen, she always seemed to know what was on my mind. From the way I ogled that box, one would think it contained the most valuable treasure in the world. And as far as I was concerned, it did. Mom knew that, and the whole treasure chest thing tickled her to no end.

"Do you want to open it to see if it's still there?"

I sprang from the sofa like a jack-in-the-box. "Yes!"

She chuckled as she went to get the key. She'd given the lock box to me especially for my cherished treasure. She used to say that half the fun of being a mother was the opportunity to experience joy vicariously through her children's happiness.

"Only twenty more days!" I squealed, bubbling over with enthusiasm as she handed me the key. "If you count today, that is."

"That's right," she said, glancing at the calendar. "Today's the first day of August."

I turned the key and slowly lifted the lid of my treasure chest. My heart skipped a beat as my eyes fell on the coveted item that my mom had ordered for me two months earlier. No, the treasure didn't glitter like gold or sparkle like diamonds. In fact, it was just a small piece of paper—a ticket bearing the words "The Beatles, Crosley Field, Cincinnati, Ohio, August 20, 1966." My "ticket to ride."

Mom had helped me organize a small party of my star-crossed friends and, after collecting the money from each *Beatlemaniac*, she'd ordered our tickets for the concert. She had even offered to drive us to Cincinnati ninety miles away. Then for the rest of the summer, she patiently endured endless hours of "Twist and Shout," "Can't Buy Me Love," and "She Loves You"—yeah, yeah, yeah. Unlike some parents, she even got into the music with us girls. But when we tried to get her to do the twist with us, well . . . that's where she drew the line.

When the big day finally arrived, she loaded us all up in the station wagon, and off we went, Beatles or bust. We left early in the afternoon even though the outdoor concert was scheduled for evening—didn't want to take any chances with the unknown such as traffic jams, wrong turns, etc. Our physical bodies may have been inside the car, but our heads were in the clouds. Mom acted like she was as excited as we were and never once did she try to stifle our state of euphoria. She even made us laugh when she shared her own personal feelings about "dreamboats" from her younger days—Frank Sinatra, Clark Gable, and Cary Grant to name a few.

"It seems girls really don't change that much from generation to generation," she said insightfully, "only the objects of their affection."

As we approached Cincinnati, we paid no attention to the darkening sky. Mom found a place to park at Crosley Field and walked with us to join the long line of fans waiting for the gates to open. She had her camera ready and took pictures of us posing with our posters and other Beatles memorabilia, all the while masking her concern about the threatening clouds overhead. She was careful not to let her fears rain on our parade, allowing my friends and I to remain lost in the thrill of the moment.

The gates opened, and the mad rush to find our seats commenced with frenzied girls (and guys) surging forward, pushing and shoving and bumping into each other. Mom waved to us before heading back to the car with yet another concern—the worry that one of us girls would get trampled in the stampede.

With one hour to spare, we found our seats. We remained oblivious to the weather until the first drops of rain fell on Ringo's drums, which had been draped with a clear plastic covering. Then reality settled in as heavy as lead. Mom was sitting in the car feeling the same way. Two agonizing hours went by, and the rain showed no signs of letting up. The announcement that the concert was rescheduled for noon the next day offered us very little consolation knowing that my mom wouldn't be able to make the trip again.

In stark contrast to our entrance, the exit was more like a funeral procession. Mom was waiting with open arms to comfort me. She said she'd been on the phone all evening calling my friends' parents and nearby hotels. There were no vacancies. And, as I suspected, she said she couldn't possibly drive us back to Cincinnati in the morning. I pleaded and sobbed as we walked to the car, but she sorrowfully replied, "That's asking an awful lot of me, sweetheart. We'll be getting home so late, and we'd have to get up so early. I just can't. I'm sorry." Though I questioned it at the time, I know now she was as brokenhearted as we were.

No one said a word on the way home. Except for an occasional sniffle, it was quiet enough to hear a pin drop. At home I cried myself to sleep. The next morning I awoke to bright rays of sun filtering through the window shade as if to mock the whole disastrous affair and me. Then, lo and behold, Mom burst into my room, grinning from ear to ear.

"Get up, Judy! We're going to Cincinnati!"

"Everyone?"

"Everyone!"

I think she'd literally been up all night wrestling with her decision to not make the trip and apparently had a change of heart. I wasn't sure what had happened, nor did I care. I just knew that Mom was determined to not let a little rain turn this memory into a nightmare. That's my mom. What a trooper!

We hit the road again singing "It Won't Be Long," none the worse for lack of sleep. We repeated the same routine we'd gone through the night before, but now the sun shone gloriously in a clear blue sky. While Cheryl swooned over George and Rosie sighed for Ringo, my heart went pitter-patter for Paul. And Mom, bless her heart, took a walk, got something to eat, and waited anxiously to see our glowing, happy faces when the concert was over.

Years later, when my own daughters swooned over New Kids on the Block, without missing a beat, Mom seized the opportunity to tease me. "Payback will be so sweet," she remarked, winking. I told her I wouldn't want it any other way, and I thanked her for being such a great mom—for creating such wonderful memories.

Oh, and Mom . . .

"P.S. I Love You."

JUDY GERLACH works as a personal assistant for her husband Greg's video production company in Lexington, Kentucky. A published author of church drama, she began her writing career writing plays and sketches for her church and has since written numerous short stories and two novels. Judy and Greg (also a Beatles fan) still enjoy listening to the old Beatles songs.

X-Mom

L. CANTOR

All mothers have three super powers: 1. The Ray, 2. The Rope of Truth, and 3. Time Travel.

When I was in eighth grade, the Internet was still a young, budding phenomenon with slow loading, confusing portals, and fledgling search engines. Using the Internet for plagiarism in school had not yet become a prolific practice, but when the facility of using it in this way occurred to me, I thought I was clever enough to be one of its early pioneers.

In truth, pulling information off the Internet and passing it off as my own wasn't necessary, or ultimately a time-saver. The process of finding, copying, and editing the right material took at least as long as simply writing a book report. But I was thirteen and perhaps simply felt like cheating—and why not? It was only a junior high book report.

The problem arose because my mother was, and remains, a writer, a prominent writer. It is well documented that she didn't have it easy growing up. My mother was born in Puerto Rico and moved with her family to New York City when she was nine years old. Because she spoke no English when she arrived, she was placed in the lowest sections of all of her classes in school. She taught herself English and went on to graduate from Harvard. Fifteen years, three books, countless awards, and some honorary degrees after that, she hosted a group of published, professional writers in her comfortable home in Westchester, New York.

In fact, every Wednesday night, her writers' group—all prolific novelists and regular contributors to the most highly respected English language publications—gathered at our house to work-shop their latest creations. Because I also had a book report due every Thursday, and because my mother thought it was a fantastic way for me to grow as a writer, I would print out a few copies of my latest draft and hand it out for a "group critique."

They gamely humored me, corrected my grammar, crossed out words like "weird" and "scorn" and changed them to "eerily evocative" and "opprobrium." The system worked beautifully; all my junior high teachers thought I was an excellent writer. In actuality, I was spoiled.

By the time I was born, my mother was no longer a *jíbara.* I was the son of well-to-do parents, living the good life in a well-to-do town, attending a private school for well-to-do kids. Despite—or perhaps because of—my privileged upbringing, or some insane urge to rebel, I thought, at age thirteen, that it was a good idea to pass a butchered copy of an old *New York Times* book review off as my own work before a panel of professional authors, all of whom likely read the *New York Times* book reviews regularly.

I brought my work downstairs to the group, passed it out, went about my business in the other room for a few minutes, and then returned to an eerily evocative silence. My mother stared down at my paper hard. When she heard my footsteps grow close enough to where she knew I could find no cover, she looked up at me, her eyes drilling straight through me. Her steady death-grip expression let me know that I had not only disappointed her, I had embarrassed myself—and by association—her. Worst of all, I'd done it in front of all of her friends. I had dishonored the family. *The Ray.*

Denial was my only option. I considered lobbing the idea that it was just a coincidence. Amazing really, that my book report mimicked almost exactly the rhetoric, tone, and rhythm of the *New York Times* book review. A testament, no doubt to how well I was taught. Yeah . . . for two seconds I thought that would work.

"Is this your work Lucas?" My mother asked, her hands gripping the pages, her voice icy, unwavering.

I silently gasped. "Well . . . "

That was all I could muster while watching, in amazement, as Mom relaxed her tense stare. Her face softened, she looked beautiful again, like the woman who would always play games with me, always laugh at my stupid jokes, always protect me, feed me, comfort me. She was my friend; I could tell her anything; she loved me. *The Rope of Truth.*

Okay, a quick apology. "I'm sorry, I . . . " but it was too late. There was no escape.

Some mothers would yell, but not mine. Her forehead tensed again, her eyes narrowed, her lips thinned, and then pursed, "Go to your room, and write *your* paper." And with those few, devastating words, I was dismissed.

I scurried to my room, but I couldn't work. I couldn't do anything but feel the shame of disappointing my mom and the embarrassment of being caught doing something that I knew was wrong. I suffered from the realization that this one stupid prank had discredited her name, all of her hard work to become a professional author, a well-respected teacher, and a first-class mother.

We never spoke of it again. She never followed up, never tried to drive the lesson home. She didn't tell me never to cheat, or even that what I'd done was wrong. But she didn't say goodnight to me that night either, though she must have heard me crying in my bedroom through the door.

To this day, when a quick way to cheat presents itself, even if it's a tiny, inconsequential, morally questionable shortcut, I find myself standing before my mother's writing group, the memory of that piercing stare burrowing into my soul. And I remember that any attempts to gain advantage through dishonesty insults what I've already been given, what my mother earned for me. I may—as everyone sometimes does—allow myself to entertain a devious plan; I may even think it through, ponder it, and even try to justify it. But as my mind travels down the perilous path that could lead to executing an act of plagiarism or deceit, I shudder. No, I literally recoil. My mother did her job—the mere thought of cheating leaves me feeling that I've earned her opprobrium. *Time Travel.*

L. CANTOR is a musician, writer, and producer. He lives in Brooklyn.

Bonjour, Mademoiselle

MAY MAVROGENIS

I t is Paris in August of 1944. The city is celebrating the liberation from German occupation. The heat in the air is not only
due to the sun, but also to the masses of people walking, running, laughing, and crying in the streets. It smells of perfume and
Gitanes cigarettes. The unmitigated joy is fueled by champagne
rescued from hiding places. A very pretty French girl is walking
her dog down the Champs-Élysées. This young woman has survived four years of hunger, fear, and confusion. The world as she
knew it was turned upside down. Now it is righting itself. She is
wearing a flirty summer dress and shoes with heels made of wood
that are a necessity of the times. A young American officer stops
to talk to her dog in fluent French. A short, "Bonjour, mademoi-
selle," and they strike up a conversation. Paulette and Marcel are
married five months later.

A year after they are married the war in Europe is over. Paulette boards the French liner *Degrasse* with her husband and their new baby. She doesn't speak a word of English. She has never traveled outside of France, and she doesn't know a soul in the United States. She comes to this country and embraces it. Maybe I shouldn't say "embrace." One of the many customs Paulette has to learn is to not kiss everyone she meets, but rather to shake their hand instead.

Marcel is a French instructor at Brown University. During the day Paulette takes care of her baby and the small apartment. She shops with her husband and starts to learn how to work with dollars and cents. She ventures out alone to make small purchases at the grocer two blocks away. Paulette points, the grocer blabbers something. She points again. He hears "Je ne comprends pas" accompanied by a smile. Somehow they both get what they want. Money is tight at first. Marcel learns the hard way that you can teach someone numbers, but it is altogether different from teaching the value of unfamiliar currency. He puts aside $100 so that my mother can go shopping for herself. He pictures her getting a dress or two and some personal items. She comes back with a $100 pair of shoes. He learns another important lesson: His wife loves shoes.

My parents and I move to Clinton, New York, where my father takes a position at Hamilton College. This is rural upstate New York. It is farm country and about as opposite to Paris culture and sophistication as one could get. Paulette does her best to fit in. The dean's wife takes her under her wing and escorts her from tea to tea, making sure that she has on her obligatory white gloves and afternoon tea dress. She learns that a cocktail party has nothing to do with birds and has everything to do with entertaining. My parents begin to entertain a lot, much to the delight of our cat, Kitty, who has a martini-soaked olive addiction.

My sister is born, and the family is complete. Our mother goes through the pregnancy and birth without the presence and comfort of her mother. She now has an infant with which to practice her English. Although it is improving, there are occasions when she is misunderstood. Such an event occurs with the laundry service that comes to the house once a week. On this particular day, she lies in wait for the laundry man. When she opens the door to let him in, he is assaulted with "You take shit. Shit go." It turns out that the laundry had not returned my mother's sheets. That particular young man never returned.

My mother decides that it is time for her to learn how to drive. Lucky for us there are *plenty* of open spaces and empty rural roads. It is the same story every week. It starts out well, and then my father makes the mistake of telling her where to turn. She keeps going.

"Je t'ai dit de tourner ici."

"Non."

My father is speechless. From the safety of the backseat, my sister and I see his baldhead getting redder. She keeps driving wherever she wants, and there is nothing he can do about it. She stops the car when she has had enough, and my father drives us home in silence. This happens every Sunday until she gets her license—her ticket to freedom.

My mother always prepares to go to the village. On come the lipstick, nylons, heels, and perfectly coiffed hair. No jeans and sweatshirt for her. Only an outfit will do. Because it is such a small town, I always receive Paulette sightings. "I saw your mother coming out of the hairdresser's." "I saw your mother at the gas station." When a local policeman makes the mistake of stopping her because she was speeding and comes to the door of the car, she starts babbling at him in French, all the while gesturing with her manicured hands. He waves her on. From that day until the day he retires, when that policeman sees my mother's red sports car coming, he just waves and smiles.

It was on one of these trips in her car that my mother comes upon baby squirrels whose mother had just been killed. They join our family. After that rescued cats and an occasional dog show up. Animals in trouble always find their way to our door where my mother welcomes them.

One of the proudest days of her life is the day she becomes an American citizen. When people hear her accent and ask her where she is from, she replies curtly, "I'm from France, but I'm an American." When someone asks if she would like to go live back home, she emphatically says, "This *is* my home."

History repeats itself. Although my mother always wanted me to marry a nice American boy, I choose a Greek foreign exchange student. I teach him how to drive. We marry and move to Greece, a country whose customs I don't know, with a language I can't speak or read. I feel no fear. If my mother can do it, so can I. My mother isn't with me to share the wonder of my first child's birth. I watch as my husband becomes an American citizen. Stray animals always find a home with me. I'm stubborn and start my sentences with "No." I zip around town in a red Miata. I grow up to be my mother. How great is that?

MAY MAVROGENIS, born in Paris, France, married and raised two children, Agnes and Marcel. She is a retired French teacher. Presently, she writes and cares for her mother who has Alzheimer's disease. Her story "Vindication" was published in *A Cup of Comfort® for Grandparents*.

Bound for Moscow

BROOKE AVED

I n 1994, when I was fourteen, a California children's theater group offered me a chance to perform in an international production of *Grease*—in Russia. My father was vehemently against the idea. In late 1993, Russian President Boris Yeltsin had ordered his Special Forces and elite army units to storm the parliament building—their "Russian White House"—resulting in 187 dead and 437 wounded. This, plus the vast unknown that was Russia, and a fear of letting his naive daughter fly 6,000 miles without a parent along frightened my father. My mother harbored fears, but where my father saw danger, she saw opportunity and adventure.

Unfortunately, the trip would cost around $3,500, and my father was the only one who could easily fund the trip. When he refused to support what he called "lunacy," and I came home crestfallen to report this, my mother squared her shoulders. "We'll find a way," she said. "Don't you worry, my beautiful, talented daughter, *you* are going to Russia."

For the next six months, she and I waged a campaign to earn money. I had always been artistic, something my mother also supported. "I could make jewelry," I said enthusiastically, and the next day we drove to our favorite bead store, where my mother plunked down $250 for beads, findings, and wire. She also helped me create promotional posters and lobby the local grocery store for permission to sell outside their doors. Week-after-week, we beaded and then spent hours in the cold night air peddling my wares. She also sold beaded necklaces, earrings, and rings to her coworkers and to friends and to friends of friends. She left no stone unturned when it came to promoting my talent for singing—and for beading.

From the time I stepped onto a theater stage at age four, my mother was the one who scanned newspapers for auditions, shored me up for tryouts, drove me to and from rehearsals, attended all my performances—including nearly eighty rehearsals and nineteen performances of *The Sound of Music* when I played Gretl at age five—and even sewed my costumes. "I'm a curtain sewer," she would say, scrunching up her nose at a complicated costume pattern. "I can sew straight lines likes a champ, but this, this . . . " Nevertheless, she tackled each project with enthusiasm and dogged determination. After days spent fashioning puffy-sleeved, full-skirted, apron dresses for *Big River*, she handed them to me beaming. "You owe me, sweetheart," she said, winking, "*big* time."

But this trip was proving a monumental challenge. The journey also required flights from San Francisco to Los Angeles for rehearsals, and my mother not only scraped together money to pay for these flights, she—alone—made all the three-hour trips to the airport and back. These first separations, which involved entrusting my safety to relative strangers, rattled her, but she did her best to hide it. "I'm going to miss you, darling daughter," she'd say, "but you are on your way to stardom and that requires travel." When it came time to release me into what she called "your waiting public," her lips would quiver until she would inevitably bite the lower one to still them. But when I turned for one last look, she would smile broadly and wave enthusiastically. "Have fun, but be good!" she'd shout, and I would roll my eyes and hope the seventeen-year-old boy who was my "flight chaperone" wouldn't think I was a baby.

Because my mother was a writer, she also created a newsletter that she mailed to everyone on her mailing list, as well as to local newspapers and social clubs. She offered news of my quest and used the newsletter as a way of soliciting donations and then thanking those who supported my effort to get to Russia. When I had to fly down to Los Angeles for rehearsals, mom reported any and all news to my fans; when I won awards for singing or was selected to sing at my eighth grade graduation, she rushed out a newsletter; when someone sent a huge donation, she heralded its arrival. Her newsletters were not simple one-page reports, but four pages of entertaining reading, photographs, and informational promotion. My mother's belief in me became obvious to all who received her work, and her enthusiasm proved contagious. Contributions were mailed; funds accumulated.

She even sent the newsletters to my father, who was not thrilled to hear that so many others were sending in money and supporting what he still saw as a dangerous dream—one he still staunchly resisted. "You are sending her into a third-world war zone," he warned, implying that my mother was being crazily reckless with her daughter's safety. Political turmoil had occurred, but my mother was convinced I could slip in and out of Moscow without incident and saw no reason to squelch what she called "a golden opportunity."

"How many fourteen-year-old girls get a chance to perform in Russia? She'll be with a contingent of fifty American students with ten adults who will watch over her every minute. The American Embassy will be very aware that they are there. They are taking every precaution." She would then smile at my father and inquire politely, "Really, don't you think it's worth the risk?"

When my father resorted to threats that he would refuse permission, my mother bristled, but she never overreacted, and she never surrendered. "You were born to do this," she would whisper when he left. "And we're not going to let his fear stop you."

In fact, at the end, my mother tactfully petitioned my father to release the $500 in my savings account, which he—finally—begrudgingly did. Without her determination, creativity, stamina, efforts, and ability to smooth his feathers, I would not have gone to Russia.

As the day approached, and my mother's fears surfaced, she coped by writing me a long letter outlining precautionary measures, how important it would be to listen to the adults, and reassuring me that I would be completely safe and return home enriched. She packed this into my suitcase so I would have visible evidence that my mother was watching over me, even while 6,000 miles away.

And so off I went to Russia, where I did, indeed, have an amazing adventure—a life experience that opened up my world and continues to affect how I view and live life. My mother had the vision to know this, as well as the chutzpah and drive to make sure I got on that plane. One of my most poignant memories was hearing the joy in her voice over a crackling wire after I happily shouted, "I spent the day at St. Basil's Cathedral!" And when I came home—bedraggled, exhausted, and immeasurably enriched—there she was, standing at the gate, waving madly, calling out, "Over here, sweetie, over here," and I ran, gratefully, into her open arms.

BROOKE AVED is a singer/songwriter who moved solo from the safe, quiet Napa Valley to the rollicking, creative Austin, Texas, to pursue her dreams of becoming "the next Sheryl Crow." Brooke's work can be heard at *www.myspace.com/brookeaved.*

Gifts from Aunt Ruthie

BONNIE BURNS

When I came to live with my stepfather's family in a small New England town in the late '40s, I was a child of the Wild West—raised in Colorado, spoiled in my early years by my doting maternal grandmother. It took many years to break me of my willful ways. My harried mother, also adjusting to a new environment, was in turn apologetic and apoplectic concerning my behavior. My new stepfather tried discipline and catechism to curb me, but it was his younger sister, Ruthie, who smoothed the edges of my tomboy soul. While my mother was distracted with her own new life, my aunt was there to transition a little girl's behavior with a motherly touch.

Most members of my stepfather's startled family gave me clear berth. My new grandmother tried, in vain, to stop me at her kitchen door, demanding that I remove my shoes before entering. Unfortunately I had already tracked mud, grass, and even worse matter onto her shining, waxed floor, whereupon in future visits I was banished to the backyard and the canopied wooden swing.

Relatives came to signify somber, Sunday afternoon visitors. Except Aunt Ruthie. Young and pretty, she wore bright colored dresses and soft cashmere sweaters. Her clothes were not the dark dresses of the other aunts and grandmothers who smelled like mothballs and cedar closets. When she sat next to me, her perfume was a perennial garden. She always smiled at me, seemingly unaware of my social transgressions, and never raised her voice, as was the habit of the other adults. Often, she sat with me in the swing and showed me how to gently pump its floorboards to attain rhythm and altitude without that exciting element of possibly tipping over. Instead, we sang silly songs to our rhythmic swing. She taught me when to wait my turn to sing in rounds; "Row, Row, Row Your Boat" and "Frère Jacques."

One rainy afternoon, too stormy for even my grandmother's heart to send me to the swing, I sat at the kitchen table (in my stocking feet) scribbling wildly in a children's coloring book. Aunt Ruthie passed by and viewing my green horses and blue trees, said, "How creative!"

The next day she gave me a Jeanette MacDonald coloring book from her childhood. The pages were filled with Hollywood fantasies, movie sets, exotic costumes, and pretty ladies. I had never seen anyone as beautiful as Jeanette MacDonald—nor anyone as dashing as her costar, Nelson Eddy. I dared not scribble in such a book. The pages were clean, and I wondered why Aunt Ruthie had not scribbled in it either. But I could not resist such a temptation. So many costumes, so many crayons. With great deliberation, I selected my colors and with careful strokes, filled the empty spaces, staying within the lines. Aunt Ruthie sat down beside me, chose a red crayon and began to color roses on the opposite page.

When I discovered the magic of words, I quickly surpassed the schoolbook stories of Dick and Jane, and I sought words everywhere. To my delight, they were everywhere. I drove my mother to distraction demanding the meaning and spelling of every ingredient on the packages in the kitchen cupboards. Each night I wanted one more story, one more Little Golden Book, but soon I knew them all by heart. I took to snitching my uncle's *Saturday Evening Post* and *Collier's* magazines even though I didn't understand much of what I was reading. When Aunt Ruthie caught me behind the sofa with my contraband, I was pleased to tell her I was reading "big stories." That Christmas she gave me my first real book. The maroon leather cover was embossed with shiny gold letters, *Little Women* by Louisa May Alcott—a book I still have and cherish. A new world opened up for me. I was still to "do time" in the swing, but I had new friends and adventures to keep me company.

Gifts from Aunt Ruthie were always special—not just because of the lavish wrapping paper festooned with huge bows and yards of ribbon. Her gifts were subtle, but luxurious hints: a delicate bottle of perfume when I balked at daily grooming, a little straw purse to encourage my weekly donation at church, a nail care kit to break me of biting my nails, and white Swiss organdy gloves when I did.

One late afternoon, I was gently rocking and reading in the swing, I looked up to see Aunt Ruthie coming down the veranda stairs, escorted by a handsome young Air Force officer in dress uniform. In the soft twilight, she looked like Jeanette MacDonald on the arm of Nelson Eddy, floating right out of our coloring book. She wore a gown of dark green taffeta with a voluminous skirt that rustled with every movement. The strong scent of her gardenia corsage hung in the summer air as she passed by. She glanced at me with a small smile, as if we shared a secret, then as she looked up at the admiring young officer, her smile burst into laughter.

That evening my tomboy soul wistfully became aware of the meaning of beauty; it was not just green taffeta and gardenias, it was grace, patience, and kindness touched with humor. I also knew that although I was not destined to be a beauty queen or a movie star, a bit of femininity would forever touch my soul. Now when I caress a fine fabric, or catch a fragrance on the wind, or swirl my skirt ever so lightly, I am again aware of taffeta and textures, perfume and poise, colors and crayons—gifts given by a gentle young aunt who occasionally stepped up as a surrogate mother to tame a wild child.

BONNIE BURNS lives once again in the Wild West after years in the big city. She still spends her time in the wide world of words: reading and writing. Although dreams of taffeta remain, her fascination is in the history of quilts: the colors, textures, and patterns of people's lives.

The Path to Hell and Gone

JUDITH GILLE

One calm, cloudy day my younger brother and I decided to pick our way through the treacherous south channel to join our cousin for a picnic on Wreck Island, a tiny provincial park on Georgian Bay, Ontario.

Many of the lake's 30,000 islands are cloistered along multifingered inlets on sheltered bays. But Wreck Island is in an area locals refer to as "the open," where the wind and waves can be ferocious. Large craft upward of forty feet are common, and few people venture out in smaller boats.

But with our eighty-eight-year-old mother serving as navigator and our three teenage daughters perched over the bow looking out for shoals, we arrived safely. Our cousin was waiting dockside.

After picnicking only a few minutes Mother jumped up and announced she was going to look for the trailhead. "I want to find that wreck," she said, charging off into the dense pine forest.

My cousin, who works with geriatric patients, looked worried. "Has she always been like this?" she asked. "I don't remember her doing things like this before."

"She's on a mission," I answered, unconcerned. "There's no stopping her."

Like all great adventurers, explorers, and archaeologists, my mother has one distinguishing personality trait: an irrepressible curiosity. Any back lake or new island located on a map must be sought out and explored. Her children and grandchildren (even her great-grandchildren) were recruited to the ranks of minions she organized for her expeditions. These were Mother's personal crusades, meager substitutes for the things she rues never having done, such as discovering the source of the Nile or the bones of Australopithecus.

My father, on the other hand, had a curiosity quotient that hovered near zero. Mother's insatiable curiosity annoyed him; his need to keep track of her verged on neurotic. This was next to impossible when she headed into the bush, a place he was determined never to go. His standard reply when one of his large brood asked him where our mother was: "She's off to hell and gone again!"

So when Mother wandered off that day, my brother and I weren't particularly concerned. But when she hadn't returned thirty minutes later and the deep furrows in our cousin's brow seemed on the verge of becoming permanent, we anteed up and feigned distress. We mustered our small troop of girls, geared up and followed our mother, once again, into the bush.

She had left a good deal earlier—with nothing in hand—while we had to pack and carry towels, snorkeling gear, two Seadoo diving tanks, and a picnic basket over the rugged terrain. We headed off in the general direction she had pointed out on a map earlier that morning. Her plan had been to blaze a trail across the island to avoid taking our boat across a rocky bay that was the site of the wreck she was seeking.

The initial path through the forest was easy, but the subsequent scrambling over granite boulders, thrashing through thigh-high juniper, and sliding on moss-covered river rock was challenging. The girls, constantly on the lookout for their grandmother, were sure we'd find her around each new bend. As we bushwhacked through overgrown forest, scaled rocky cliffs, and stubbed our toes fording stony streambeds, my brother and I began to ask ourselves: Could our octogenarian mother really have gone this way?

Yet we persevered. Exploring is in our blood. Our small expedition was intent upon finding the wreck and, hopefully, our mother.

Forty-five minutes later, we reached the small beach where the skeletal carcass of the wrecked steamship lay just off shore. But when we saw no sign of Mother, a deep uneasiness overcame me. Leaving the others to snorkel in the shallow waters, I climbed to the top of a granite precipice. Scanning the landscape for my mother's petite frame, the terror I had once felt as a child, chasing her through a tangle of creature-infested bushes, rose in me like tiny bubbles from a lake bottom.

* * *

It had been a thick, steamy day in August 1959 when my family, *sans* Papa, had been picking blueberries and lunching near Moon Falls. Then, as now, Mother had decided to scout out yet another lake she remembered from childhood. Then, a nervous six-year-old with an overactive imagination, I had constant visions of becoming snack-food for a black bear. So instead of obeying my mother's instructions to stay with my siblings, I had mustered my courage and scrambled off in pursuit of the only person with the strength to protect me from this disagreeable demise.

Not having inherited my mother's navigation gene, I quickly lost track of the path and began wading through a tangle of juniper bushes and berry brambles, snagging my shorts and scratching my legs. The oppressively humid air of the mid-August day and my impending panic made it hard to breathe.

Suddenly, a rustling in the bushes twenty feet away startled me. My heart began to thump fiercely in my chest and the tiny, sun-bleached hairs on my arms stood on end. A loud *crack!* punctuated the hot, silent air as a dry branch snapped in two.

"Maaama! Where are you?" I screamed, desperate to conjure up her presence. The small crumb of courage I possessed had quickly vanished. I began to blubber loudly.

"Cry-baby!" my older brother snapped, surprising me from behind, swatting at me in an effort to shut me up. "You should 'a stayed with us, like Mom said."

Suddenly, our mother came crashing through the brush. "I found it! I found the lake, just where I thought it was!" she said triumphantly.

So here we were again, in search of our wandering mother. My brother and I felt a familiar relief when, after scrabbling back via the same rugged route, we arrived exhausted at the dock to find Mother, in her swimsuit, lounging on the boat deck. Her clothes were spread to dry on the canvas top. The persistent breeze we'd been hiking against had pushed the clouds southward, and the sky was brilliant.

Our girls shed their burdens and ran to greet her.

"Where have you been, Grammy?"

"I hiked out to see the wreck, just like I said I would," she answered, sounding pleased with herself. "Where have you been?"

"How the heck did you get back so fast?" my brother asked.

"I hitched a ride with a boat full of teenagers. They couldn't very well refuse a nice old lady."

"Fooled them with the nice old lady routine, eh? They don't know how dangerous people like you can be," I replied—only half joking.

It wasn't the onset of Alzheimer's that made my mother wander off. She has *always* done it. And I hope she always will. For there's no place in the world my mother would rather meet her Maker than on the path to hell and gone.

JUDITH GILLE is a freelance travel writer who, like her wayward mother, has spent a lifetime of summers exploring Georgian Bay.

Her Second Language, First Love

SANDRA BRETTING

The kitchen smelled earthy and raw that summer's day, of salted chicken simmering in a hearty broth—the kind of smell that conjures a Kansas farmhouse, not a cliff-side dwelling perched high above the Pacific Ocean.

"Soup? It's ninety degrees outside!" I said dismissively, as I sauntered into my mother's kitchen.

"I'm reading *The Grapes of Wrath*," she patiently replied. "It's what they ate."

Of course. Whenever my mother delved into a book, its fictional characters could become as real as our next-door neighbors to her. She liked to embody their imaginary lives. From Steinbeck's downtrodden to the arctic survivors of a Jack London story, so great was her love of classic American literature, she willingly endured imaginary travails and rejoiced in make-believe triumphs.

As a teenager, I often wandered into her paneled library, kept just off the kitchen. A filled-to-the-brim, eight-foot-tall bookcase spanned the length of the room. An equal opportunity reader, my mother had placed dog-eared copies of the *Reader's Digest*—a decade's worth—beside beloved hardcover texts by F. Scott Fitzgerald, Ernest Hemingway, and Mark Twain.

To her credit, my mother never nagged my three siblings and me to join her on her literary safaris; she merely kept the means and motivation close at hand. A plump leather couch faced the bookcase, perfect for nestling into after retrieving something—anything—to read. A brass and wood wall clock patiently ticked off the seconds, gently syncopating words as they appeared on the page. In the distance, waves crashed into the coast of Dana Point, or was that the seashore beckoning from Michener's *South Pacific*?

In my mother's library, adventures called from behind every leather-clad spine, and oddly enough, they became a safe pier from which her children navigated the churning waters of adolescence. Really, how bad could an algebra assignment be when poor Kunta Kinte faced daily beatings in Alex Haley's *Roots*? So, everyone else had a date to homecoming? At least we didn't have to weather the stench and struggles of Steinbeck's *Cannery Row*. Maybe our best friend had let us down, but she wasn't nearly as bad as the tortured souls in Poe's "The Fall of the House of Usher."

Ironically, the keeper of these great American works wasn't even born in this country. My mother is Dutch, and she grew up conjugating verbs in her native tongue, as well as German and

French. As a schoolgirl, she switched languages as easily as most American children change clothes.

But after watching Hitler decimate her neighborhood as a child, she became determined to immigrate to America. Years later, savings in hand, she arrived in Canada, where she promptly enrolled in night school. While the rest of the young ladies at the YMCA drank highballs and danced "The Stroll," she would trudge over the icy streets of Vancouver to the library with English textbooks wedged in her coat for safekeeping.

She finally became a citizen of the United States after she met and married my Dutch father, and together they journeyed to California. Throughout that time, she never missed an opportunity to improve her English. When I was young, she dutifully enrolled at Cerritos Community College. If it bothered her to be the only mother in a class full of bored twenty-somethings, she never complained. If she would rather rely on her native tongue, like so many of the immigrants we knew, than struggle for the exact English word, she never let on. If it took a month's worth of grocery money to buy a set of the *Encyclopedia Britannica*, we were none the wiser.

Her hard work paid off in unique ways. My siblings and I excelled at book reports, homework essays, and even the annual spelling bee. One year, I had the honor to be the last child left standing at my elementary school's bee. But lest I think my mother took this event lightly, my father showed me his reddened hand in the foyer of the building afterward. Seems my mother had dug her nails into his skin so deeply, channeling her nervous excitement onto his flesh, that he suffered crescent-shaped scars for days afterward.

While no mother is perfect—who among us is?—mine instilled in her children a love of language and a deep respect for the written word. Her legacy is something I rely on each day as a journalist for the *Houston Chronicle.* Because of her, no matter how bad my day might seem, a massive whale still trolls the Gulf Stream, a bull rages through the streets of Pamplona, and lions troll the Serengeti as Ernest Hemingway patiently awaits my return.

SANDRA BRETTING writes for the business section of the *Houston Chronicle* for money, and short stories for literary journals for fun. She's also scattered books strategically throughout the bedrooms of her own two children.

A Century of Courage

SOPHIE LEVINA

When my mother, Rebecca Dubovsky, was age eighteen, she walked day after day along ruined railways in Western Russia, heading east, equipped only with her backpack containing a mug, soap, dried bread, and a change of underwear. Civil war, famine, bandits, and misery raged that fall of 1919. Sporadic shooting and explosions could be heard far and near. Shuttered hotels and eateries meant she slept on wooden benches in half-bombed railway stations or sought shelter in abandoned ruined houses.

Rebecca had graduated with distinction and was intent upon becoming a physician to relieve human suffering. Even though physicians were among the lowest paid professionals in Russia, medicine was her chosen vocation, her devotion for life. The medical school in Warsaw would be the nearest to her hometown Pinsk, but they did not welcome Jews, so Rebecca and her closest female friend resolved to journey about 1,000 kilometers from Pinsk to Moscow, where they had heard Jews after the revolution of the 1917 were (unbelievably!) as welcome as anyone else.

The journey stretched over two months. Midway, Rebecca's friend, unwilling to tolerate ever-escalating dangers and hardships, grew weary, and chose to return home. Wise as it might have seemed at the time, it equated to a death sentence: On Yom Kippur in September 1942, during another gruesome war, the Nazis massacred her entire family, her neighbors, and her fellow townsmen in Pinsk.

Never one to surrender, Rebecca had continued her journey alone—incurring a series of mishaps and sidestepping danger throughout. Once she had missed the local train she had been on. Because conditions were abominable, tea service was no longer available. Passengers would disembark when a train paused at a station and make a mad dash with their kettles to fetch boiling water. Rebecca had just filled her kettle when her train suddenly chugged and sped away—with her backpack in it. Rebecca had no money, no food, and no identification papers. Desperate, she cornered and quickly recruited a local farmer who drove her to the next station. For the rest of her life, recollection of that day resulted in overwhelming heart-stopping panic. It repeatedly haunted her, in her waking hours and her dreams.

Another time, she had squeezed into a rear open part of a train car (she never dared to enter inside as she had no ticket). Unfortunately, soldiers packed the car and several watched as she climbed on board. One of the soldiers ordered Rebecca off the train, and when she resisted, grabbed Rebecca's backpack and angrily tossed it to the ground. The train started moving and although she panicked—her backpack was all she had—trains were irregular and unreliable. She could wait for days, or even weeks, for another opportunity.

Luckily, before she had to make the crucial decision whether or not to jump, another soldier leapt down, grabbed the backpack, and was back up on the car in a split second. "Anyone who harms the girl deals with me!" The solder bellowed this as he squared his body against the steps, protecting her.

When the train arrived in Moscow and Rebecca found her way to the State Medical School, they welcomed her, but also informed her that a dormitory would not be available for a month. She stumbled out onto the street, aimlessly walking, feeling abject, totally at a loss. Suddenly, miraculously, the very soldier who had rescued her stood in front of her.

When she told him what happened, he once again came to her rescue. "You will stay with my mother and sister," he insisted. "I have to go back tonight to my military barracks, but you will stay." Rebecca agreed, as long as she could repay them as his sister's tutor in math. Some time after Rebecca had moved into a dormitory, the soldier proposed, but Rebecca declined, and they never met again.

When Rebecca learned that the State Medical School requested a uniform, she felt desolate. Would her dreams die because she couldn't afford to buy a uniform? They agreed to a "dress code" consisting of a white top and a dark bottom. Rebecca didn't have a white blouse, and even if she could scrounge up enough rubles, the store shelves were perennially empty. After all her efforts, to be turned away for the lack a blouse was unthinkable. Rebecca suffered for days until she came up with an ingenious idea. She would trade her month's worth of bread coupons in return for her roommate's spare white blouse. The students' daily ration consisted of a small portion of bread and a bowl of thin cabbage soup. For a month, Rebecca survived solely on watery soup.

Somewhat fortuitously, when winter came (because the school could not afford to heat the auditorium) professors and the students alike wrapped in coats, shawls, blankets, or whatever they could find to keep them warm, concealing—and thus nullifying—the required white top. Not only had Rebecca managed to survive in an unknown, unheated, and starved Moscow, but six lean years later she graduated from the State Medical School, again with distinction. She worked as an internist for the next forty-nine years. It was, indeed, her call; many times she had been told that she was "a doctor by God's grace." Later, she earned the rare title "Distinguished Physician."

Rebecca taught Internal Medicine at the Moscow Medical School for twenty-five years, and during World War II, served as a Major of Medical Services, working in a hospital for wounded soldiers. Rebecca was awarded war medals for her contribution, but when Stalin enforced his virulent anti-Semitic campaign (1948–1953), she and her husband were abruptly fired because the distinguished doctor and her husband both "had a brother in Israel." Rebecca went on to conduct medical research and earn a PhD in medicine. She also published many research papers.

In 1980, Rebecca immigrated to Canada with her daughter's family. Well into her nineties, she volunteered to teach Russian and serve as a book cataloger in the library of the International Center in Winnipeg. When she passed in 2007, at the ripe age of 105, she left behind a world of inspiration.

SOPHIE LEVINA was born, educated, and also worked as an MD in Moscow. Like her mother, she obtained a PhD and Doctor of Science in medicine and conducted medical research. She has published more than fifty research papers and two monographs. After immigrating to Canada in 1980, she worked as a MD for another twenty-one years.

Lessons Learned up a Tree

CHUCK HOLMES

I didn't want to be a coward. I didn't want to cry in front of Dan Gilbert and Richard Britt. But most of all, I didn't want to fall out of the pecan tree. I crouched on a big limb, hugging the trunk of the tree as tightly as my six-year-old arms could stand.

I had tried to turn loose. Dan and Richard had both been up, then down the tree and couldn't really understand why I had a problem. They kept telling me that going up was the hard part.

"Just put your foot on the next limb," Dan yelled. That was easy for him to say. He was standing on the ground. I was about twelve or fifteen feet up in the air and just one breath away from falling and splattering myself all over the ground. I noticed that Dan and Richard weren't standing directly beneath me.

For four or five minutes things didn't change. Dan and Richard kept encouraging me to come down. I kept hugging the tree. I could tell from their faces that boredom was setting in. It probably wouldn't be long before they left me, and I would be there, up the tree, maybe just providing food for some big birds. Just the thoughts of it made me cry more. I rubbed the tears from my face with my shoulder. I wasn't about to let go of that tree trunk.

"Maybe we ought to go get his mama," Richard said. Dan considered it for a minute. It looked like he was trying to decide if I was worth the extra effort, but the three of us had been best friends ever since we could remember, and they probably didn't want to just leave me there. Besides, Richard's daddy would have used the razor strap if he knew that Richard had left his best friend to die.

I closed my eyes as tight as I could, and then opened them again, hoping that something would have changed. But it was still the same, except that Richard and Dan were running off in the direction of my house. I just hugged the tree tighter and cried some more.

At some point between squeezing my eyes shut and opening them again, my mother appeared directly under me. Dan and Richard stood just behind her, well out of the way in case I fell. Mother was looking up at me with a puzzled expression on her face.

"How'd you get up there?" she asked.

"I climbed up here," I sniffled. "Dan and Richard climbed up here, so I did too."

Mother turned and looked at Dan and Richard standing behind her. They shrugged.

"Do you think you can climb down?"

Even at six I didn't consider that a reasonable question. If I could have, I wouldn't be crouching on a limb hugging a tree trunk. I just shook my head and tried not to look like I was crying. I wasn't very successful.

Mother kept looking at me; then she took a deep breath and grabbed the first limb of the tree. She pulled herself up. Standing up, she stepped on the next limb. She climbed up until she was sharing my limb. I noticed that she didn't have to hug the tree to stay on the limb. I supposed that had something to do with being a grownup.

She pushed her hair back and wiped a bead of sweat from her upper lip.

"I haven't done this in a long time," she said, looking around. I looked, too. Everything was fuzzy through the tears, but I could see a long way. "When I was a little girl, I liked to climb trees. I just liked to be up where I could see a long ways off."

She pulled a tissue out of her pocket and wiped the tears from my cheeks. I felt better, knowing that she was up there with me, and I knew that she could get me down.

"Help me get down," I said.

She shook her head. "Uh-uh. You got into this situation, and you're going to have to get yourself out of it. That's just the way life works."

I started to cry again. My mother was my last hope, and she wasn't going to help. I could feel the tears running down my cheeks. I was about to go past crying into sobbing.

She wiped the tears from my cheeks again and put her hand on my shoulder. "Here's what we're going to do," she said. "I'm going to take a step down, then you're going to take the same one.

I'll show you how it's done, but you have to do it yourself. Think you can do that?"

I considered my options—or my lack of options. I nodded my head. I had to get out of the tree somehow.

"Okay," she said, "Just remember, I'm right below you."

She grabbed a limb and stepped down to the limb below. She stood there, waiting for me. I finally released my bear hug on the tree trunk and grabbed the limb she had used. Then I eased myself down to the one she was standing on. She went down to the next one, and I followed. Finally we got to the bottom limb, and she stopped.

"And this is the fun part," she said. "For just a second you get to fly." Then she jumped off, and stood under the tree, close enough that she could have taken me in her arms. But she put her hands behind her back and looked up at me with a big smile on her face. "Now, let's see you fly."

I knew that my mother would never tell me to do something that would hurt me, so—despite the fact I didn't think it was a good idea—I jumped off the lowest limb and found myself on the ground, perfectly safe. Mother helped me dust my pants off. Then she went back to the house, leaving me with Dan and Richard. We were equals again. I had climbed up and—more important—down the tree.

CHUCK HOLMES has been a writer for fifty years and has never found any of the many things he learned from his mother to be more useful than the lesson he learned from her up in the tree: You get yourself in a situation, you have to get yourself out of it. And the people who love you are not far away.

Courage Comes in a Small Voice

LYNDELL KING

Helene lived next door to my rundown childhood home. The short, dumpy woman kept mostly to herself, owned a savage Alsatian guard dog, and spoke mainly in German. Many of the neighboring Australian housewives viewed her with slit-eyed suspicion, if not downright hostility. Even after two decades of peace, post–World War II bitterness tainted their opinions, yet I never once saw Helene treat others with anything but an endearing, shy kindness.

We first met when I was ten and practicing for a Goethe verse speaking competition. I had to memorize a poem in German, and my mother suggested Helene might help with my pronunciation. I suspect Mum seized on any opportunity to get me out of her hair for a while, but I was just as happy to escape the household bickering. I soon spent every evening at Helene's kitchen table, sharing her family's meal. She'd proffer food while pronouncing its German name, and then insist I answer in perfect German. Faulty pronunciation meant food was momentarily withheld. Delicious food. So I learned—fast—twisting my tongue around the guttural language in exchange for spicy sausage and cinnamon-apple strudel. As our friendship grew past the language barrier, I shared with her some of the problems I suffered at home and how worthless they made me feel. Helene shared about her past too. What an education!

She'd been born in Nazi Germany, the child of German farmers who sympathized with the Jews during the Holocaust. When her parents helped the Jews hide from the Nazis, they brought Nazi wrath upon their heads. At age eleven, the Nazis separated Helene from her family and sent her away on a standing-room-only train, never to see her loved ones again. *Never.* She spoke haltingly of the brutality she experienced—of having her gold earrings torn from her lobes, of gold teeth being callously ripped from her mouth, of rape and starvation, and of all manner of inhumanity that made my own troubles seem suddenly smaller.

I often sat at her feet, wide-eyed and amazed that her life had been so cruel and yet she'd remained gentle and loving. Even though the war was long over and she was *safe* in Australia, her life was far from easy. She battled daily with a grouchy, needy, diabetic husband and two macho, demanding teenage boys. She also lived in a community that neither understood nor befriended her, leaving her to privately endure a sense of displacement and staggering loss, not to mention horrific memories that must have kept her up at night. Yet there she sat across the table from me, sweetly offering whatever help I asked for—and more—with no talk of payment or debt. Amazing—and a sort of motherly kindness I had never known before.

Going to her home every day after school, I soon learned I wasn't the only one she helped. She had a weakness for stray cats, birds that fell from their nests, the homeless, the hurt, or the downtrodden—anyone or anything that needed her. She'd creep in, do her good deeds, and creep out again. Mostly no one even knew of her good deeds. No one, but me, seemed to be watching. To a child from a dysfunctional home who daily saw how ugly people could be to each other, Helene, alone, appeared heroic, and I wanted to be like her.

A few years later, when I was thirteen, my brother and sister (who I later learned were really half-siblings) left home, and my Mum fled the coop too, leaving me behind with an angry, alcoholic gambler (who I later learned was not really my father). Even though we both felt abandoned, my pseudo-father took his anger out on me, and he often let days pass with no food in the house.

I never mentioned this to anyone, but as if she could sense when I needed her most, Helene would peek over the fence and ask nonchalantly if I could use a cake, or a piece of meat, or whatever else she'd been cooking. "I always cook too much, and I hate for it to go to waste," she'd say, shrugging her shoulders as if implying foolishness. If it hadn't happened so often, I might have believed her. She knew I was too proud to tell her what was happening, so she found her own way to care without embarrassing me. And how I loved her for that.

She saved my life in those days, and not just by feeding me. When my family cast me off as if I was yesterday's garbage, she had a completely different view. "You're so much better than they think you are. Shoot for the stars. Even if you only hit the moon, you'll come out shining." She'd deliver this message with a smile and end by dipping her head to peer into my eyes. In doing so, Helene gave me something vital: She gave me hope.

I had big ideas in my youthful mind of finishing my education and buying her a huge, lavish gift as a thank you for all those years of selfless giving. I almost felt cheated when she died before I could execute my plan, but that's because I didn't really understand her until lately. The whole point of the love and forgiveness she showered on everyone was that she gave it freely. She never used it as manipulation to make us behave a certain way. Her kindness, courage, and generosity were just there, shining and true, part of her character. Helene modeled real courage—the courage to experience some of the most horrific pain life can deal and solemnly declare, "I choose to be soft and sweet and caring despite it all."

I'm now a mother grappling with the daily frustrations of raising two semi-rabid boys. I try to keep their goals high in the starry heavens, and teach them that, more than all the awards or jewels or money or prestige the world can offer, Helene's grace is a prize well worthy of gain. One day in the hereafter, I hope to once again look into Helene's kind eyes and tell her what her brand of courage has meant to me, about the many times when life dealt me more than I felt I could bear, and how the memory of her kept me from hardening my heart into a pool of bitterness. I want her to know that I still aim for the stars, but it's the love, courage, grace, and hope Helene gave me that warm me up and let me shine.

LYNDELL KING lives in Tasmania, Australia, with her husband, two homeschooling sons, and a variety of animals both domestic and wild. (Though none so wild as her kids.) She writes full time and publishes romance under the name Babe King.

Easy as Pie

PAULA MUNIER

Patience will achieve more than force.—Edmund Burke

Fudge. Chocolate cake. Pralines. My mother makes it all—and more. Dropping by my folks' house is like visiting your favorite bakery. Only better, because Mom greets you with the confection of your choice. For her grandsons, it's cheesecake. For her granddaughter, it's cinnamon coffee cake. For me, her beloved only child, it's brownies and pecan pie.

My mother is Martha Stewart on speed. Anything Martha can do, my mother can do better—and faster. She's in her seventies now, but that doesn't keep her from enveloping the people she loves in warm, sweet hugs of sugar, sugar, and more sugar. Just as English mums believe that there's no problem a cup of tea can't help solve, my thoroughly American mom believes that there's no problem dessert can't solve.

But only if it's made at home with loving hands.

When I was a young woman in my twenties, I asked my mother to teach me to make pie. Up until that point, I don't think I'd ever asked my mother to teach me to do much of anything. I thought that everything I needed to know I could learn from my father. The Colonel was the one who was out and about, doing important things with his life. Mom was his cheerleader—and mine—tending the home fires with the patience of Penelope while her own warrior husband saved the world. But instead of weaving, Mom baked. As a teenager, my greatest fear was that I'd end up like my mother, living vicariously through my husband and children while baking batch after batch of Mexican Wedding Cookies. Coming of age in the seventies, when women's liberation was changing life as we knew it, I was impatient to conquer the world, not feed it.

Once I married and had children of my own, all that changed. The same woman I had once secretly regarded with an affectionate condescension, I now regarded with an astonished admiration. Nothing I had conquered in the so-called real world had prepared me for the demands and challenges of motherhood; only my mother held the secrets to the maternal arts I struggled to master. She could quiet a colicky baby, entertain a bored toddler, and whip up Mickey Mouse pancakes all at the same time. She never appeared tired, or frustrated, or cranky. She never raised her voice or let a swear word slip or even rolled her eyes. She was as unfailingly kind and cheerful and patient tucking the kids in at night as she had been sixteen hours earlier greeting them at breakfast.

Such strength, such organizational skill, such discipline! As it turned out, the Colonel's wife was as clever and commanding as her husband, if not more so . . . who knew? I realized that my adoring mother had more to teach me than I could ever learn. Worse, I was afraid that with my temperament I might prove congenitally incapable of learning it. So I decided to start with something easy: pie.

"The secret to a good pie is the crust," my mother told me. We were in her kitchen, a happy place full of light and love and real vanilla. She assembled the ingredients before us: two cups flour, cold water, two-thirds cup Crisco, salt. She poured the flour into a clear glass mixing bowl, tossed in the salt, and spooned the Crisco on top.

Then she went over to the sink and washed her hands. "You, too," she said to me, drying her hands. I washed my hands, and she passed me the towel.

"Okay, now watch." Mom started cutting the Crisco into the flour with her long, elegant fingers. "Now you try."

I stuck in my hands and manipulated my digits in imitation.

"That's good. Now when it's down to a mealy consistency, it's time to add the water. Some people use 7UP, but I prefer water." Mom took out a measuring spoon and handed it to me. "Four to five tablespoons should do it."

I added the water and formed the goo into a ball as instructed.

"Time to roll out the dough." Mom sprinkled flour on the kitchen counter and floured my hands as well as her own. Then she took a rolling pin and rubbed flour along it. "Flour the ball of dough and flatten it with your palm." She watched as I slapped the dough down, nodding. "Nice. The trick is not to work the dough too much." She gave me the rolling pin. "Now roll it out and put it on the pie plate."

I rolled and rolled and rolled, but my crust remained too thick here, too thin there. Time and time again I tried to lift the dough onto the pie plate, only to have it crack and fall apart. "It's impossible!" I was prepared to throw in the towel.

My mother laughed. "No, it's not. All you need is a little patience."

"That's just it, Mom. I am not a patient person." Nonplussed, I ran my sticky fingers through my hair. "I am not patient like you. I'll never be as good a mom as you."

"Nonsense." My mother looked at me. "You're wonderful with the children."

"But I'm not patient."

"You are patient enough." Mom pointed to the dough. "You can make a good pie crust. Try again. Take your time."

I sighed and once again flattened the ball with my palm, once again rolled out the dough, once again lifted the doughy circle onto the pie plate. This time it remained intact.

"I knew you could do it." Mom smiled at me, and showed me how to fit the crust into the plate, and mark the rim with a fork. "That's the hardest part. The rest is easy."

And so it was. That day, my mother taught me the art of making a good crust. More important, she taught me that if I just took my time, I could learn patience. I would never be as patient as my mother, but I would be patient enough. And then the rest would be easy.

Easy as pie.

PAULA MUNIER is director of innovation for Adams Media. She is also president of the New England Chapter of Mystery Writers of America. Her stories and essays have appeared in numerous anthologies. She successfully raised two children and currently lives in Pembroke, Massachusetts, with her son Mikey, two dogs, and a cat. Her pies are legendary.

My Son's Other Mother

LAURA-LYNNE POWELL

Without her, I never would have heard my son's first word, celebrated his first step, or witnessed his pride when he pitched in his first Little League game. Without her, I might never have become a mother. She is my son's first mother, the teenager who gave him his life—and then gave him to me.

Emergency surgery for an ectopic pregnancy had left me unable to conceive, and efforts to become pregnant through invitro fertilization had failed. I reluctantly turned to adoption, even while worrying almost incessantly about the power it gave the other mother over my future and that of the child I hoped would become mine.

My husband and I traveled across the country to be interviewed by a pregnant woman considering adoption, but we retracted our hopes when she openly smoked marijuana. Our grief was still raw when another woman we had met during the trip telephoned to tell us she had just learned her teenage daughter was pregnant.

Kim was a popular high school sophomore and athlete who had fallen in love with a boy a year older and become pregnant the night she lost her virginity. She was considering adoption as the best outcome for her baby, a boy. Her mother asked us if we'd like to meet her.

Once again we flew across the country and nervously prepared to meet a stranger who would decide if we would become parents. My fears were allayed as soon as I stepped off the plane. The sixteen year old greeting me at the gate with a bouquet of flowers was not my adversary. Kim was a vulnerable girl in crisis seeking the courage to do what she thought was best for herself and her baby. Her mother welcomed us with warm hugs, while Kim offered a shy smile and a gift—a baby's photograph album and a card on which she had written, "This is for holding your memories."

After two days of long talks and lengthy walks in the park, we were all in agreement and said goodbye with tears and kisses. We talked on the telephone often during the five months that remained of Kim's pregnancy, staying abreast of each stage and monitoring her resolve. Kim sought to reassure me, but when she told me she crooned country songs to her unborn child every night and liked imagining what he would look like, I knew she was experiencing doubt. But I also knew she wanted what was best for him, and I did my best to trust the mothering instincts that were also growing within her. I felt confident Kim would choose whatever she felt most strongly was best for her son and hoped that choice would lead to me.

But a knot of fear remained, even after her mother called us to report that Kim had gone into labor. I knew Kim's resolve was about to face its biggest test. My husband and I boarded the next plane and entered Kim's hospital room feverish with emotions that swung from terror to joy.

Kim cradled her newborn and smiled with motherly pride. As I approached her bedside, I heard her whisper to her son, "Meet your new parents." My stomach literally flipped, and my throat tightened as she placed her baby in my arms. A priest Kim had summoned performed a baptism as Kim, her parents, siblings, and my husband and I quietly wept. Kim said goodbye to her son by placing one last kiss on his forehead.

We decided to keep the name she had given him—Christopher.

A few months after returning home with our son, Kim sent us a song about a pregnant girl who was convinced that adoption was the right choice for her. On the cassette box, Kim had written, "It says everything I mean. Please listen to the words! You can play this song as you rock Christopher to sleep at night. I love you."

Kim grieved for a long time. Sometimes she still does. But in our phone calls and letters, she insists she suffers no regrets. The life she chose for him with us was one she couldn't offer at the time he was born. She's proud of the family she helped create.

I celebrated every childhood milestone with Kim in mind. I whispered my gratitude to her as I played tooth fairy, mailed Christmas lists to the North Pole, and joined other mothers in a tearful huddle outside the kindergarten room door on the first day of school.

I cheered when Kim's high school graduation notice arrived in the mail and again when she graduated college. I showed friends at work pictures of her wedding and recently posted photographs of her two beautiful sons on our refrigerator door.

Thirteen years have passed, and I am still grateful for Kim's grace and kindness every day. Kim not only allowed me to become a mother, she has continued to love the boy we both adore without ever making me feel less his mother by doing so.

Recently, when Christopher suffered a sudden serious illness, we alerted family and friends—including Kim. While I was able to stay in the hospital, glued to his side night and day, Kim worried frantically and did the only thing she could—she prayed.

When Christopher recovered, Kim sent me a note, mother-to-mother, saying simply, "Our prayers have been answered."

Yes, they were, darling girl—thirteen years ago, and every day since.

LAURA-LYNNE POWELL is a writer and mother living in Sacramento, California, with her family. Her second son's birth mother, Andrea, is also one of her lifetime heroes. A member of the Writing Mamas, Laura-Lynne's work can be viewed at *www.writingmamas.com*. She is currently writing a memoir on becoming a mother through open adoption.

Mormor

NADYA SUSTACHE

My mother travels through four different airports—alone—to meet her newborn grandson.

Twenty-four hours after her departure, she arrives at the Swedish city of Gothenburg and proceeds to baggage claim to retrieve her bulging suitcase. She comes prepared with everything her grandson *may* need: diaper rash cream, liquid Tylenol, teething rings, bibs, bottles with a box of rubber nipples, white socks in multiple sizes, tiny summer sandals, and six graduated pairs of leather booties.

She walks on blonde wooden floors, her shoes going clackety-clack as she makes her way through the deserted Customs area. Although baggage handlers aren't clamoring around eager to help (as they are in her native Puerto Rico) she prefers to strain her arthritic wrists than pay for help anyway so pushes her suitcase outside and hails a taxi. She hands the driver printed directions, slides onto the leather seats, and soon recognizes the road signs that lead to Högsbohöjd. When they arrive at her destination, she pays the driver and thanks him (in English with a Spanish accent). At the door, she picks up a key hidden underneath the welcome mat. Inside, all is quiet. She stands still a long time, unsure what to do next.

Somewhere else in the city, I am in a taxi with Stefan, my premature son. A white-suited *barnmorska* (baby nurse) and I sit on either side of his basket. We have just departed the hospital where he arrived six weeks early. The plastic tube that we must use to feed him mother's milk—some of it pumped from my breast; the majority of it provided by the hospital's milk bank—is taped inside his tiny nose. We are journeying to a neonatal unit at a different hospital where we hope to teach Stefan to nurse.

Once there, we enter an eerily quiet room—as quiet as a library, except here five mothers sit wordlessly attempting to breastfeed their infants, whispering requests for help only when needed. At 3 P.M. a *barnmorska* lights the Advent candles, and I notice that the world outside has turned to night—a night that will last eighteen hours. When Stefan sleeps, I retrieve my journal, fervently hoping that the act of writing will distract me—from the incessant worrying about an underweight, fragile Stefan, my dwindling milk production, and my mom.

My mom is a woman of courage and determination, but she lives in the tropics. She came here once, in summer (with my father), but nothing has prepared her to welcome a cold, dark Swedish December alone. I must wait here, with my newborn son, frustrated that I cannot help her cope with the vastly unfamiliar freezing temperatures, icy sidewalks, and the long night ahead. They will unnerve her, and I'm not there to help her, or to explain how to do basic things like make a phone call, operate the European washing machine, or read food labels.

Hours pass. When I arrive home—alone—we hug, sighing in silent relief. The house is newly clean and orderly; a hot meal waits on the table. "Don't worry," she says, "This is not a leisure trip. I've come to work." But I am so filled with worry my stomach churns and tightens, making it impossible to eat—and impossible to lactate enough to meet my small son's needs, to fill the pump I must clutch repeatedly to my chest instead.

Later that night, once again at the hospital, my mother greets her grandson from the other side of the glass entrance door, where I stand opposite, holding him. The neonatal unit refuses to let my mother enter, even after I tearfully recount that my mother has traveled thousands of miles. Surprisingly, anger surges, unstoppable beneath my surface, but I suppress it. This cannot be the way my mother wanted to meet her grandson, nor is it the way I had envisioned it. I long for her to be able to touch his soft skin and smell him the way I can. The smiles on our faces conceal our mutual disillusionment.

Two weeks pass. I spend most days and nights at the hospital. One *barnmorska* after another teaches me every trick in her lactation arsenal, from the application of sprays designed to induce hormones to painful nipple attachments, but Stefan will not latch onto my breast.

At home, my mother does all she can to help. The house is clean, the fridge is full, and my husband's ironing is done. She has a bus pass and a map of places to visit, but she ventures no farther than the closest grocery store. Although she tries to deny it, the whims of light in this northerly latitude rattle her. Gloominess, mirroring that of the outside, assaults her usual cheerfulness. As I know too well, twinkling Christmas lights and abundant decorations do little to brighten the oppressing winter darkness.

New Year's Eve arrives, and I complete *Breastfeeding 101* with a failing grade. Stefan still isn't mastering the art of holding on and letting go, and I'm barely generating sufficient milk to meet his needs, let alone fill the unending parade of pumps. The *barnmorska* prescribes the dreaded bottle and reassures me that nature will take its course at home. I thank everyone at the hospital (in Swedish), snap photographs, and jot down their phone numbers—just in case.

Once home, Stefan and I finally strike the delicate balance, and he begins to *suga* my milk from my breast. Nature works its magic, but I am well aware that my nascent motherly instincts are equally due to nature and nurture—my mother's nurture. My mother not only taught me the gentle art of holding on and letting go, she traveled thousands of miles, deep into the winter darkness, to gift me with her presence, knowing wisely that I would need her. Once we are safe, she leaves on January 17th— Stefan's original due date.

Twenty-four hours later, my mother greets my father at the San Juan airport. He waits—flowers in hand—eager to take her home. In the car, my mother does not bemoan the bitter cold, the long nights, the endless worrying, and the ongoing frustrations. Instead, she tells him how lovely it felt becoming a grandmother in Sweden, enthusiastically explaining that each grandmother acquires a unique name—*mormor*, mother's mother, or *farmor*, father's mother.

M*ormor*, a word that is as simple and precise as it is beautiful, will forever be a reminder of the first days my mother and I shared as *mor* and *mormor*.

NADYA SUSTACHE recently published personal essays in *North Shore* magazine (December 2007) and *Chicago Parent* magazine (September 2007). She is currently at work on a memoir entitled *Blue Eyes, White Lies*.

Strong Fingers

BILL ELLIS

Miss Edith grew to just under five feet tall and a hundred pounds and always said, "They ran out of parts when I came along." But she was her daddy's favorite and earned his highest praise of having strong fingers when she played the piano. While her older sisters preferred housekeeping and cooking to help their mother, Miss Edith climbed an apple tree and read a book.

One question pummeled me daily growing up in Martinsville, Virginia. "Say, are you Edith's boy?" Questioners asked when the resemblance in my face didn't quite jive with my six-foot, two-inch frame. Next, most said, "Lord, where did you come from? Your mother is the tiniest woman." Showing my manners, I laughed with them.

Everyone knew my mother, Edith Hailey Ellis, because she was secretary to our congressman and ran his real estate and insurance business. "Ran" is the correct word because no one doubted who the boss was. The men in the office would say, "Miss Edith will take care of you," and this applied to handling late paying renters, hiring contractors to fix rental properties, and writing up insurance policies. Mom handled it all because she was the only one who knew how.

She typed all correspondence for the "old" senator, and later for his nephew who inherited the business. Yet *typed* isn't the correct word. I learned this while waiting in her office for a ride home. One day the nephew dictated for forty-five minutes, and luckily Mom took shorthand. Nevertheless, I dreaded how long it would take her to type this malarkey. Worse, it was near closing time when the loquacious dictator stopped talking and left.

"You have to finish that today, Mom?"

"Yes," she answered with a sigh. "He's put it off too long already, and now he'll be out hunting quail for days and I'll never catch him."

"But doesn't he have to sign it?" How would she locate the man out in the fields? But Mom was busy typing, fingers flying over an old manual keyboard. Finished in a couple of minutes, she zipped the missive from the platen, read it, signed it, and showed it to me. I was astounded. The letter was one paragraph of five lines!

"Mom, he said a lot more than this. Won't you get in trouble?"

"He said a lot. But this is what he meant," she replied.

An even greater signal of her anomaly surfaced when she taught me how to drive. I watched her technique closely, trying to discover how she did it. I wouldn't need the seat and back cushions she required to reach the steering wheel. Neither would I have to stretch my long legs, as she did her short ones, touching the pedals tiptoed. And as awkward as this may sound, my mother was the best driver I ever saw.

"How did you become such a good driver, Mom?" I once asked her.

"I drove Mr. Burch all over Virginia when he campaigned for office from 1930 on," she said. "He was glad to let me because he was a terrible driver, just like your father." We both laughed. Dad was plain awful; I was afraid to ride with him. And I could visualize Mom driving around the state acting as chauffeur, secretary, and campaign manager all in one. Bottom line: Men in her life recognized she did things better and had the good sense to let her alone.

Leaving church service one morning, she looked miserable. "The preacher claimed I made a mistake not staying home to raise you," she said. True, the man had spoken of the recent revelation that children learned crucial values and knowledge from age zero to six, but it never occurred to me that anything he'd said applied to Mom, and I told her so.

I recalled she'd taught me good manners, to respect other people, to act like a "southern gentleman," to say please and thank you, and above all not to be a hypocrite. This last teaching came from her years in Washington observing life on Capitol Hill. Yet my words did not soothe her feelings. Guilt remained because her older sister had been called in to "handle" me shortly after I was born. Mom was terrified she'd drop me. After hiring Tessie to care for me, Mom went back to work. We kept Tessie for eighteen years, the last dozen or so because my father loved her cooking.

During confirmation hearings for several of President Clinton's political appointees, "Nannygate" surfaced. And too many of Mr. Clinton's selections had to drop out because they had not paid Social Security taxes for their housekeepers. Naturally, it seemed a good question to ask Mom about Tessie.

"Yes, I paid those taxes, and Tessie retired on Social Security." About Mr. Clinton, she said, "Not presidential." Who was the best president in her lifetime? "Truman, because he stuck to his guns. Oh, but Daddy would roll over in his grave if he knew I'd ever voted Republican against Clinton."

Mother lived with my wife Joan and me after her second husband died. In one conversation, I asked where she wanted to be buried.

"Well, I feel bad with your father all by himself back in Martinsville. But all the folks I knew back there are gone. Can't go to Richmond; Jack has a spot for me next to him, but his first wife is on the other side. I really want to be beside Daddy in Keysville. But Cousin Betty buried her husband in that spot. So I don't know where to go."

"Why don't we have you cremated, and Joan and I can sprinkle your ashes all over Virginia. Little bit in Richmond, Keysville, and Martinsville." She clapped her hands, and we both started laughing so hard tears ran down our faces.

Entering the clinic for a medical appointment, she could be heard clear down the hall singing a hymn. Spotting me, she smiled, recognizing me only in that place as her son. Spying a downcast fellow across the room, she announced, "That's my husband over there, but I had to get rid of him." The reception room laughed as one. With a lifetime goal to outlive her parents who died at eighty, she persevered to ninety, laughing and singing the whole journey, near the end of her life in her own language.

Even her death certificate contained dry humor. When I read that the main cause was "global geriatric decline," I burst into laughter and said to no one in particular, "Shoot, Mom would have said she just plumb wore out."

BILL ELLIS has published two novels: *Second Chances* in 2001 and *Leading Voices* in 2004. He has mentored at-risk students for AmeriCorps and served as writer-in-residence at Sunset Middle School in Longmont, Colorado, coaching "critters" in publishing an online magazine. Learn more about Bill on *www.billelliswrites.com*.

A Patch of Sky

M. CAROLYN STEELE

The child of a mail-order bride and a Polish sea captain living in Alaska, Mama was naturally daring, occasionally outrageous, and never ordinary like other mothers. At least that's what I thought when I was seventeen. We had moved, again, this time from Texas to Oklahoma, with everything we owned in the backseat of our old car.

"Is that one?" I asked, nudging Mama's shoulder. We were lying face-up on the front lawn. She rolled her head close and sighted along my outstretched arm into the vast expanse of sky and stars. The hint of vinegar she used to rinse her hair wafted through the air.

"No. It's bright, but it's only a star." She patted my hand. "Remember, a UFO will move fast until it decides to hover over something. We'll be lucky to see one"

Lucky was something we weren't, but Mama never quit hoping.

A ragged cloud moved into view, and I found myself wishing really hard that a spacecraft would come hurtling through it for Mama to see. "Would it be bullet or saucer-shaped?" I asked, resurrecting the previous night's conversation.

"Boomerang."

"Like kids play with?"

"Sure," Mama answered, making a V-shape with her fingers. "A V-shaped vehicle with the pilot in the forward point would make the best spacecraft. In a saucer the pilot would have to sit in a bump on the top. That doesn't seem like it would make for good vision possibilities. What do you think?"

I didn't have an answer. Maybe something would come to me the next day while I did chores, waiting for her to come home. Then, we'd spread our favorite spaceship gazing quilt on the lawn and pick up the subject again while Mama rested her blistered and bruised feet, after eight hours of working in a store.

"The sky here seems smaller than the sky in Corpus Christi," I said wistfully.

"It's because of the big trees, Honey. They hem in your view and make you focus on a smaller area of the sky . . . rather like nature's telescope." She took a deep breath, and I wondered if she missed the smell of gardenias as much as I did.

The cloud vanished, and soon thereafter a flash arched directly overhead—a bright, thrilling, unexpected shooting star. Mama sucked in her breath. "An angel just sneezed in heaven," she whispered. "Now, that's good luck."

I lay down next to Mama, hoping for another sneeze.

"Do you hear it?" she asked. "That old oak is whispering to us right now."

I stole a quick glance toward the side of the yard where an oak tree reached several stories high. Its rustling leaves sounded like muted chatter, and I found myself wondering why the trees would want to talk to people. What on earth would they say?

Mama leaned over. "The Indians consider the trees their standing brothers, you know. They believe that when a man no longer has the strength to stand, his tall brothers will hold him up."

Mama could do that—change the subject in a flash, retrieving knowledge, blending fact and superstition to make something interesting. She kept me off-balance, never quite sure what was real and what was just a story. Sometimes I wondered if she knew the difference.

I trained my eyes on the heavens. The leaves still rustled, but seemed to quiet, as if they knew I was now really listening for them to say something. "The trees must be talking in Indian, Mama, because I don't understand a thing they're saying."

"Pancakes, Honey."

"They're talking about pancakes?"

"Sure," Mama said and rose up on one elbow to look at me. "Listen harder. They think we ought to have pancakes for dinner." She pursed her coral-red lips, lifted a finger to them, and shushed me. "If we're really quiet you will hear them."

"If they're saying we should have pancakes, I guess they don't know we're out of syrup . . . and bacon."

For a moment, Mama's smile faded, and I wished I'd kept my mouth shut and played the game like I always did. It wasn't her fault that we couldn't afford syrup, or bacon.

"Well, then," she said finally, smiling again, "we'll have to eat our pancakes like the Europeans do, with butter and sugar sprinkled on top."

"Europeans sprinkle sugar on their pancakes?" I stood and held my end of the quilt while she folded it toward me.

"Sure, they also eat snails dipped in garlic butter."

I looked at Mama, trying to decide what was true and what was her overactive imagination. She lifted her eyebrows, daring me to top that one. Who could top snails in garlic butter? "I guess I'd rather eat pancakes with sugar." I took the quilt from her, scanning the sky once more.

"Thought so," she said, limping toward the back porch. "They'll taste good, you'll see."

Mama was right. Stirred together with a bit of this and that, flavored with mystery, and topped with butter and sugar, the pancakes tasted good. Caught up in her imagination, I forgot about the missing bacon and syrup, forgot about the stack of unpaid bills and the days left until payday. Mama fed me legends, mysteries, world happenings, and discussions about what we'd do with all the money she'd make when she sold her novel.

We kept our vigil almost nightly, even in winter, waiting for UFOs that never appeared. Once, bundled in coats, we lay shoulder to shoulder, staring into a black sky curiously void of stars. That night even the trees grumbled, snapping, and groaning in the cold.

"Wait and see," Mama urged when I grew impatient. "On a night like this, something wonderful might happen."

"The trees don't think so," I replied, and Mama laughed, her breath sending delicate puffs of smoky whiteness into the air.

Directly above, a tiny spot appeared in the dark, its shape softening as it spiraled toward us. Mama pointed a slender finger—her signal for the heavens to open up—and in an instant, hundreds of fat snowflakes tumbled down, landing on our cheeks, coating our eyelashes, and kissing our outstretched hands.

"Like magic," Mama whispered, breaking our enraptured silence. Even the trees had grown quiet. "Can you imagine," Mama asked, "each snowflake has its own design? Like people, no two snowflakes are alike."

Mama was right. This was better than seeing a spacecraft. Better even, than being in Texas where it didn't snow.

Years later, I learned the real reason for Mama's rich fantasy life. Her childhood had been shrouded by tragedy. Born Melba Kent Kalkins, she had witnessed her mother being murdered, contracted tuberculosis, and suffered serious bouts of depression. When she finally told me those stories, I finally understood why she had filled my childhood with stories about guardian angels,

Indian lore, magic, superstition, UFOs, and space aliens. My extraordinary mother shielded us both from life's harshness and daily disappointments in a hundred small ways. She used diversion and wonderment to relegate our poverty to the corners, and then filled the center with hope and dreams.

M. CAROLYN STEELE became a writer to fulfill a promise to her mother and has had short stories published in a number of anthologies. After her senior year in high school, Carolyn resolved to never move again and still lives in Tulsa, Oklahoma, where she has yet to see a UFO.

Eggshells

AMY REYNOLDS

I struggled with self-inflicted horrors throughout my teenage years, daytime nightmares and midnight pitfalls. Every day I sank deeper into a widening abyss, struggling to get a grip on the reality I used to know. Basically, I tortured myself. And when the emotional pain I couldn't understand or handle became overwhelming, I transformed it into physical pain I could control. Cutting, slicing small slivers of flesh until tiny rivers of bright red blood flowed from the wounds became the only way I could find solace—or at least some weird release that no one understood, not even me. I couldn't explain that I felt simply and completely lost—unreachable, untouchable, and utterly unlovable. I was incommunicado, sans voice mail. Nobody was home. I didn't believe anyone else deserved to share what I felt, to experience the pain I had caused, so I pushed everyone who'd ever mattered to me away and created a massive wall no one—not even my mother—could breach.

Yet, no matter how much I protested, my mother proved immovable. I pushed, and she stood firm; I fought, and she held her ground. Because we were both equally stubborn and bullheaded, we faced an insurmountable standstill. Even though she was clearly heartbroken by my intractability, she absolutely refused to walk away and thus took the only path available—to walk on eggshells around me, to wait me out. At first, it backfired. The more my mother treated me with kid gloves, the more depressed and angry I became. I felt incompetent, weak, defensive, and scared. My self-created emotional prison felt dark and cold, like I was trapped in the emptiest time of my life. No matter how lonely I felt, no matter how much my mother tried to intervene, I refused to let her love in, to let her shine new light on the situation.

Some days, I felt as if I would literally choke on the bitter words that seemed to spill from my mouth, hateful words directed toward the only person who refused to give up on me. Some days, I silently begged her to crush the eggshells, to screw being careful, and to slap me hard across the face. Even in the midst of my turmoil and blustering rage, I knew that if anyone could shake me up, wake me up, and bring me back to life, it would be my mother—the woman who had given life to me in the first place. But somehow I could never find the words to tell her what I wanted, needed, and yet could not accept.

Even in the darkest days, my mother surely knew I was on the brink—that it could have taken a fatal turn—but she dealt with it by standing by, keeping one eye solidly on me at all times. Her faith in me, her persistence, her undying, unconditional love, her wisdom, and her strength eventually won out. Even to me, the arguments, the slamming of doors, and the irrational name-calling grew tiresome. Eventually, sheer exhaustion took hold. I simply couldn't bear being alone anymore.

Our aggression slowly ebbed, leaving behind a new, palpable silence between us. My mother would open her mouth as if to speak, and then close it again, withdrawing the unspoken statement I longed to hear. I imagined plucking an emotional proclamation from her lips—a profound statement that would not only repair the damage my depression had caused, but would finally snap me out of the cold and bitter mental state that tormented me. Oddly enough, those words never came. Instead, a misshapen miracle revived us.

Crouching on the cold linoleum floor of our cramped, dingy bathroom at dawn while waiting for the indicator stick to turn blue felt far from miraculous. It felt horribly treacherous, particularly for someone who still teetered on the edge. But there I sat, barely seventeen and about to learn I was indeed pregnant. I dreaded telling my parents, particularly my mother. But when I worked up the courage to do so, I was astounded that she never overreacted, never sobbed or cried hysterically, never berated or scolded me. My mother did not waste a single breath telling me what a huge mistake I had made. She didn't point out that my choices up to that point had been those of a child. She merely, calmly said that my choices would now be "adult choices, focused on the welfare of the child."

Later, as we sat together quietly, she gently pulled her fingers through my hair, brushed it from my face, and tucked it behind my ear, the way she had comforted me as a child. "This child will be to you what you always were to me," she said softly, sweetly.

"A pain in the ass?" I said, sighing, stealing a furtive glance at my mother's face. She looked luminous, kind.

"No," she replied, scrunching up her nose and kissing the top of my head. "This baby will be your best friend."

Throughout my pregnancy, my mother never harbored or displayed icy tones of hidden resentment. Unlike others, I never once sensed a feeling of shame emanating from her. I felt ashamed, but this was my doing. None of it came from her. Instead, my mother often seemed serene and often smiled a half smile that conveyed both the sadness she felt about my lost innocence (and the challenges that lay ahead) and the happiness she knew we would all soon feel. If I accused her of being melancholy, she would simply say, "There is no time for regret." The gentle way she said this healed our wounds, smoothed the scars, until slowly, almost without noticing, the depression that had colored my life for so long lifted. Soon that simple declaration, her attitude, her sentiments, her strength—offered precisely when I needed them—became a credo I would embrace.

My mother and I had an unspoken understanding. We knew that many teenagers—and their families—would view pregnancy as the end of the life they wanted to lead. But, for me, we knew this pregnancy would become the beginning of the life I had so long denied myself. My mother knew this before I did. When she cried, her tears reflected the joy of knowing that I now had something to live for—someone beyond myself to nurture, protect, and love. In a perfect world, I wouldn't have had a baby at seventeen, and my mother would have gotten the daughter she deserves, one who was happy and healthy, one who went to college, one who married before she started a family. But in my perfect world, my mother wouldn't change. The mother I always wanted is the mother I already have.

AMY REYNOLDS is an aspiring writer and mother of two splendid miracles. She lives in Big Bear, California, with Zoey and Caylee—the lights of her life.

Mom the Riveter

BRUCE B. RUTHERFORD

When I heard her open the front door and leave, I didn't need to look at the clock. It was always precisely 5 A.M. She had a half-mile walk to the bus stop, followed by an hour's ride, changing busses twice before arrival at Pratt and Whitney, an airplane engine manufacturer. Although I didn't connect that name with her until many years later, during the height of World War II, my mom became one of the women known as "Rosie the Riveter."

All I knew in sixth grade was that she dressed differently than other moms, which tended to embarrass me, particularly when my classmates pointed it out constantly. Walking to school, I reassured myself by whispering under my breath, "What did they know?" Just because their mothers dressed in skirts or dresses and wore pointy shoes while mine went to work with a bandanna wrapped around her head and heavy work shoes on her feet didn't make them any better than my mom.

Many times I longed to tell them an impressive story about my mom, but I knew they would think I was lying. Someday I'd work up the courage to say, "Yes, with Humphrey Bogart."

And they'd say, "Who?"

I'd exclaim, "He's a movie star, dummies," looking at them like they were from the moon or something. I knew if they listened, they would be jealous of me and perhaps finally get over the way she dressed.

The story was true. Mom had danced with Humphrey Bogart once. She showed me his picture on the front page of the *Hartford Times* at a bond rally for the war. She told me he played a lot of gangsters in his movies, but when she asked him for a dance, he was very gracious, "He took my hand gently and remained a gentleman the whole time," She would say wistfully.

She was singing with a group she formed on her own at a speakeasy in the days of Prohibition. She saw him walk in with a number of people, mostly women. The manager escorted him to a front row table. As she sang, Mr. Bogart kept catching my mother's eye and tipping his drink glass at her as if to say, "Nice song. How about another one?" When their last song finished, she whispered to her group, "I'm going to ask Mr. Bogart for a dance."

She stepped down from the stage, strolled over to his table as if she had known him all her life, and asked, "Mr. Bogart, will you dance with me?" One of the women at his table reached over and touched his arm, a gesture of *are you sure you want to do this?* He eased away from the table, signaled the band to strike up a tune, said, "Call me Bogie," led my mom to the dance floor, and away they went.

Mom said, "I don't remember my feet touching the floor."

I never did tell that story, but in the long run I didn't have to, because one day our teacher announced that our class was going on a field trip designed to help us realize what sacrifices the home front was making to help win the war. We didn't care if it was to the zoo, to the museum, or listening to the mayor talk about saving paper for the war effort. Anything beat conjugating verbs for a day.

We scrambled onto the school bus, trying to get a window seat, or to sit next to the girl who let you carry her books home yesterday. As the bus rolled away, our teacher stood up behind the driver and said, "Class, today we are going to a factory where they make airplanes. The very ones that fly over Germany dropping bombs on the enemy." Most of the boys on the bus shouted excitedly and began making airplane engine noises, mimicking machine guns, or puffing out their cheeks before blowing out bursts of air to sound like exploding bombs. Mrs. Lundgren, our teacher, finally shouted above the clamor, "Boys, boys, quiet down, please."

One hour later, we passed through a gate guarded by a Marine sentry who greeted us with "Welcome to Pratt and Whitney." *Mom's factory* I wanted to shout.

Inside the noise was overwhelming. We could hardly hear the tour guide as he led us through parts of the factory. Everywhere we went he shouted explanations of what was taking place at each stop. All we could hear were interspersed words over the noise:

". . . propellers that . . . here are . . . these parts make up the . . ." until we stopped at a large metal door that seemed to stretch as long as a football field. The guide pushed a red button, and the door slid open, revealing a huge metal cage bolted to the floor. Inside the cage was an airplane engine fully assembled, with its propeller attached.

We squeezed inside the room, and when the noise quieted down, our guide said, "This is where the final engine is combat tested. All the requirements for the engine have to be exactly correct, or we return it to be fixed. This is the most important step because from here if it tests properly it will be assembled on the B-17 bomber." All the boys knew what the B-17 was: "The Flying Fortress," the workhorse of the bombers.

The guide handed us protective earmuffs, turned to the cage, and signaled to a person standing by ready to test the engine. We swung our gaze forward, and there—with her finger on the switch—stood my mother. She caught my eye, hit the switch, and the engine thundered into life. The cage shook back and forth so hard I could feel the floor vibrate beneath my feet. Some of the class backed away toward the door. But my mom remained calm, intently monitoring a large panel of lights that flashed on and off. She clearly knew what she was doing and carefully recorded her observations on a pad.

After a few minutes, she shut the engine down and moved toward us. "Hello, class. That was a brief demonstration of our engine check. We have to do more, but I wanted to show you how the engine is checked and prepared properly for combat. Thank you." She caught my eye again and gave me a sly smile.

On the bus going back, my heart strained against my chest with pride as my classmates exclaimed how lucky I was "to have a mom like that." Jumping down from the bus back at the school, I vowed to someday tell them about "Bogie" too.

BRUCE B. RUTHERFORD is a retired Marine aviator and former chair of the department of English at the United States Naval Academy. He holds a master's degree in arts from the University of Connecticut and found his second act teaching English at Sandhills Community College in Pinehurst, North Carolina.

The Power of the Pen

ERIC REITAN

On Saturdays when I was eleven, Joe would come by unannounced, pulling into the driveway in his VW Rabbit, and he'd take me to his office.

My mother asked about it, of course, about what we *did* there. I told her about the skeleton, the microscope, even the cadaver with its chest cut open and numbers inked into the formaldehyde-scented flesh. I mentioned the ritual trip to the vending machine for hot chocolate. I didn't mention the *Playboy* magazines, a retrospective collection through the '60s and '70s, or how we'd leaf through them together, how Joe would talk about the tits on that one, the ass on the other.

Joe was a family friend, a neighbor, and a professor at the medical school. My parents trusted him enough to ask him to babysit when the usual high school girls were unavailable. But I knew better. Not that I understood what he was. Now, looking back, I can see the trajectory of our Saturdays. It's with revulsion that I recall the time he showed me his sperm under the microscope. At the time, it was only with fascination. His furtive preparation of the slide was just a prelude to looking at something cool.

But I knew, even so, that our afternoons together were a secret thing, and my eagerness for the *Playboys*—and the *Penthouses*, and eventually the *Hustlers*—kept me silent. Joe had found his own patient, calculating way to ply me, at the bud of puberty, with sex. Perhaps it's only in my memory that his gaze was hungry.

It all stopped, abruptly, before it ever reached what I now see as the just-about-inevitable conclusion. It stopped because my mother was watching more closely than I knew, and she saw into the silences. And then she acted, in her own characteristically quirky way.

My mother was born in Norway, a preacher's child, but she spent her formative years trapped in Denmark under the Nazi occupation. And so she has a Danish streak. She lives in broader strokes than her Norwegian siblings. She wears bolder patterns and brighter scarves. While she was a docent at the local art gallery, she was sought after for her contagious enthusiasm, for the ringing voices of the school children she inspired. But the Norwegian reserve still lingers.

The 1970s were not a time when stories of molestation were the fodder for twenty-four-hour cable news coverage. There were no Lifetime movies of mothers daringly facing down their children's molesters with baseball bats and righteous rage. On the surface, at least, it was a more innocent time. No one really wanted to expose what was hiding underneath. It was certainly not the sort of thing a Norwegian immigrant—steeped in rules of privacy and reserve—would do on mere suspicion.

But my mother had her Danish streak. And she loved her children fiercely.

"What do you *do* there?" She asked it every time I returned. She'd look over as I stomped into he kitchen, a towel on her shoulder or a wooden spoon in her hand.

"We look under the microscope at stuff. He's got a real brain in a jar!"

It's educational. I willed her to believe it, so I could have my hour leafing through the *Hustler* spreads with trembling fingers.

"What else?" It was her usual followup. But once she asked it an extra time. And I looked at her, and I saw in her sharp blue eyes something powerful.

Perhaps some part of me understood the truth, and I spoke out of self-protection. I minimized it all, of course. In my telling it was a few *Playboy* magazines, old ones I'd found on a low shelf in his office, which Joe let me leaf through while he did other things.

But the confession was enough. "Tell him," she said, "that I'd like to see one."

"What?"

"One of those *Playboy* magazines. I've never seen one. I'd like to."

It was an elegant response. She didn't shame me or give me reasons to wrap myself in deeper secrecy. She launched no accusations she could not substantiate. She set up no prohibitions that I'd predictably defy, hungry for the forbidden pages, for the heavy breasts and bleached hair and furtive smiles. Instead, she asked for one of the magazines.

And so I passed the request on to Joe.

We were in his office, *Hustler* magazines strewn out between us, the room laden with my own amorphous, preadolescent desires, with Joe's darker ones, with our mutual impatience for different kinds of culmination. The new *Hustler* had a scratch-n-sniff centerfold, and the absurd warning: *Absolutely not to be sniffed by minors.* Joe dutifully scratched the circle between the woman's thighs, sniffed it, and invited me to do the same. But the warning was there, and it seemed more real, more forceful, than any of the warnings on the magazine's cover. It seemed in that moment that to sniff it would be to cross a line into something dark, an end to childhood.

And so I refused. And Joe pressed, understanding perhaps that this was the tipping point, that if I gave in now, to this, other things would follow. And so I thought about my mother's request.

"My mother wants to see one of your *Playboy* magazines."

The words were a hammer on ice, cracking the opaque thickness of it. I knew that everything was abruptly different. Suddenly, there between us, amidst all the open pages and their crude images, stood my mother.

In that moment my adolescence veered back to safer paths. I felt relief, even as my eyes looked wistfully across the pages, the intimations of things I longed for but didn't understand.

I came home with a *Playboy* under my arm, which I handed to my mother. The next morning it was sitting on the kitchen table. She'd gone after the smiling model on the cover with a ball-point pen—drawing circles around the naughty parts along with marginal notations ("Ooh la la!"). And the magazine's price was circled in exactly the same way. "Joe," she'd written in her curlicue script. "Two dollars for *this*? It ain't worth it!"

The woman on the cover had been turned into a cartoon. I was mortified. The blue ink had scribbled over my feverish desires, revealing them as the tawdry things they were.

She returned the magazine to Joe that day. For several weeks after that, I waited around on Saturday afternoons for Joe's car to pull up, even though a part of me understood he wouldn't come. And then, without drama, my Saturdays became again about my orange bicycle and the place the kids in the neighborhood called *mud hills*, where a pond and a forest had resisted the developers.

The truth is that sometimes, when mothers save their children, nobody knows but the child. And even the child doesn't see it until years later, when a few bold strokes of ink start to look like a map leading home.

ERIC REITAN is an associate professor of philosophy at Oklahoma State University, specializing in ethics and philosophy of religion. He has a few short story publications, including "Faerie Storm" in the *Magazine of Fantasy and Science Fiction*. His is also the author of a nonfiction book, *Is God a Delusion? A Reply to Religion's Cultured Despisers*.

Prophetic Stories

R. GARY RAHAM

"Did you ever have your palm read?" I asked, stealing a furtive look at my hand.

Mom smiled. "Once, at a carnival." She looked at me with her lips pursed a little, her eyes lidded with mischief. "Just for fun."

Looking back, I wonder if she was ever surprised to have given birth—at the age of thirty-nine and after several miscarriages—to such a solemn little boy, particularly one so intent on asking annoying questions like: "If God made the universe, then who made God?" Someone who, even at the tender age of ten or so, knew that palm reading belonged with the myths of Santa Claus and the Tooth Fairy, but who often wondered "what if . . .?"

Had I been a little older, I might have wondered if she'd discussed palm reading with my brother and sister, both nearly two decades older. Bob demonstrated a bit of her mischief and inherited a fair share of her athletic skills. Mom had always wanted to be a P.E. teacher, but relatively few women of her generation—even those wild and crazy Roaring Twenties flappers—fulfilled such aspirations. Besides, her chronic asthma ended that particular ambition. Joy mirrored my melancholy style, sometimes broaching depression, but she balanced that with Mom's perception and compassion.

"So what did the palm reader say?" I prodded.

"Well my lifeline's pretty long," she said, pointing to a crease that snaked up my own palm. "I see yours is, too."

I squinted my eyes. Who could tell? I saw a pretty major epidermal intersection near the bottom there. What was that supposed to mean? "Who dreams all this stuff up?" I asked.

Mom just shrugged in that way she had. One side of her mouth "quirked."

"What else did he say?" I suspected she was holding something back.

"Well," she continued, "he did say that *I* wouldn't be famous, but that one of my children would."

Now that proved to be a conversation stopper. I had two older siblings, but they were *way* old—staring thirty right in the withered old face. Guess whom that left to make a prophecy come true?

Of course I didn't believe in that kind of stuff.

My dad's influence by itself might have turned me into an accountant or businessman of some kind. There's nothing wrong with that. I admired Dad and worked alongside him many years flipping burgers and deep frying donuts at the family diner. My brother, in fact, did become a CPA and outearns me (and outplays me in tennis) to this day.

There's *almost* nothing wrong with that. Besides, he never learned how to cook.

But Mom somehow Yinned some of my dad's practical Yang enough that I suspected I could do something more. She wrote poetry to celebrate life's little occasions. She knew instinctively that comic books and science fiction wouldn't permanently rot my brain, and she could look the other way and wink sometimes. She tolerated bugs and frogs and stroked my leatherback turtle's chin until, I swear, it almost purred. She knew that dreaming wasn't a waste of time.

When I couldn't think of anything else to do with my scientific and artistic obsessions, my mom didn't stop me from becoming a biology teacher, but neither did she object when I married the P.E. teacher, nor when I quit herding seventh graders to look for some sort of vague fulfillment as an artist. (And Freudians be damned for whatever you're thinking about the P.E. teacher. She just happened to be a cute and ornery female colleague.)

I'm not famous, by the way. No one has ever dropped a tomato (or thrown one) in the grocery store when they saw me or tried to rip my clothes off. You won't find my image on T-shirts or my voice on the radio. And I'm certainly not monetarily rich. I've written a few books and gathered some modest recognition for my creative efforts. I bought a refrigerator magnet once that says boldly: "Almost Famous." That's close enough.

My wife and I raised two daughters successfully. I didn't tell them a story about palm reading, but I did paint them into pictures now and then and wove bits and pieces of their lives into narratives that spanned space and time.

I hope that was enough for them.

I now have grandchildren with their mother's eyes, and some have "quirks" lurking at the corners of their mouths. None have asked me the Big Questions yet, like who made God and such, but they won't be long in coming.

I've told them the story about how a wealthy aunt unofficially adopted my mom and raised her in the United States to improve her chances for a full life. I've shown them pictures of her at their age now, picking her nose in front of a store in Manchester, England, in 1912. I've told them that her fellow schoolchildren used to give her a penny to hear her talk with that funny English accent and that, if she were still alive, she would like nothing more than to give her great grandchildren pennies to hear their thoughts. I've shown them a smiling little girl with bangs and a white dress and, not surprisingly, their smiles have mirrored hers.

But I'm still looking for just the right story to tell them: something improbable, tainted with the hint of mystery—

a story in which they can don the hero's cape and perhaps fulfill a prophecy.

They don't have to believe the story. They do have to believe in themselves.

R. GARY RAHAM becomes almost famous visiting middle school classrooms and convincing eighth graders that paleontologists and artists lead fun and exciting lives. He also writes an assortment of books, articles, and nature columns proposing that nature's book is a funny and worthwhile read. You can see his particular take on science, art, and nature at *www.biostration.com*.

Steel Wool

VENUS DE MILO GAULT

My mother was a stunner. Youthful and petite, she had the body of a supermodel. Even her nurse's uniform looked couture on her small frame. She had long auburn hair that she wore in a simple chignon. Her skin was void of almost any color, and her brown almond-shaped eyes disappeared behind her high cheekbones when she smiled. She resembled a young Lena Horne. So graceful and elegant, she was striking.

She also took great pride in everything she did. The house was always immaculate; meals were always lavish affairs; shoes were always polished; clothes were spotless and carefully pressed. Mama was fastidious, so of course she took great care in keeping me "looking presentable."

On Saturdays, we tackled my hair. Mama would gather all the necessities: rattail combs, bush combs, grease, shampoo, clean towels, rubber bands, hairballs, and other odds and ends. After assembling everything, she would lead me into the living room—

a dim room with a massive brown sectional, a brown and orange shag carpet, and dark wood paneling on the walls. My mother would park herself in "Daddy's seat"—the premium seat in the house because it had the best view of our oversized floor model TV. No matter, we weren't there to watch TV.

Instead, the agony began. My mother clamped my little body between her surprisingly strong limbs. Even though slender, Mama had surprisingly taut thighs, and she wasn't averse to using them when I squiggled or squirmed. We began by untangling whatever intricate hairdo I had at the time. Usually braids, beads, or a gnarly combination of both. This alone seemed to take an eternity. Slowly, methodically, she unraveled one strand at a time, carefully undoing what had taken hours to create during her last creative burst.

While taking down each braid, unwinding three strands of crinkly hair, being mindful not to tangle the hair or create knots, tossing my head to and fro like some rag doll, pressing my chin so hard to my chest that I thought my sternum would break, and snatching my earrings out of my ears by carelessly combing too hard, the only words she spoke were, "Turn yo' head this way. Turn yo' head that way." And to make it worse, what she said and what she actually wanted me to do weren't necessarily in tandem. She was sneaky too. Her voice was always so calm I sometimes underestimated her threats to whack me with the comb. And sometimes she would. Oh yeah, I remember that well; that and my butt getting tired and sore from all those hours held captive on the hard living room floor.

When all the braids were undone, I followed my mama to the kitchen where she would pull up a chair to the sink. I would climb up to the sink with some assistance from Mama and then stand there, patiently staring at the yellow curtains with their ugly brown flowers. They somehow matched the avocado green Whirlpool stovetop and the harvest gold Amana refrigerator that mama covered with what she called my "masterpieces." Directly above the sink, mama had a spice rack that held spices nobody bothered to use. Mama was a purist. She used salt, pepper, and maybe a little garlic salt when she was feeling festive. Behind the sink, a plastic backsplash designed to resemble stark white brick was uneasy on the eyes, but fun to play with. I would poke a "brick" until it would pop back, making a wonderful sound.

Mama ran the water until it reached the optimum temperature, and when it was hot enough to bother me, she put her hands firmly on my scalp and guided my head to the basin. I would lean over and let the faucet rain down over my bushy crop of wild hair. Water whispered over my ears, telling me secrets I no longer remember. It seemed to coo to me, comforting me like a mother does her child. My mama's bony, diligent, persistent, determined fingertips massaged my scalp, mashing whatever shampoo she had bought on sale through my thick, tangled hair. Every few minutes, she shook my head hard, as if convinced the harder she shook, the cleaner the hair. To Mama, cleanliness *was* next to godliness. She shook so hard, suds flew everywhere. My eyes rolled around in my head, my brain knocked against my skull, and I laughed. Strangely enough, at some point it had started to feel good—or at least ridiculous.

But abruptly, Mama forced my head under the faucet and turned up the volume until a rush of water, along with my mama's fingers, combed through the length of my hair. Water cascaded over my hair root to tip, baptizing each strand, seeping into every nook and niche of my tresses. When all the suds were gone, Mama gathered up my hair, rung it out like it was a wet rag, and then briskly wrapped a towel around my head, cinching it tightly. All of this was done the way she did everything, meticulously and vigorously.

Back in the living room, with me once again lodged between my mother legs, she would shove my chin to my chest and start at the back of my head, stretching my shrunken hair back to its normal length by parting, untangling, and applying medicated original formula Sulfur8 anti-dandruff hair and scalp conditioner to my head. It smelt like bug spray and stung so sharply I wailed. "The burning means it's working," she'd hiss. You couldn't blame Mama, combing my hair equated to combing steel wool. Sometimes halfway through my hair, after a few seconds of tugging on a knot, combs flew out of Mama's hand and ricocheted through the living room. And, folks, this went on until late into the evening.

Bless her, my mama tried really hard, but the outcome was always mediocre at best. Come Sunday morning, however, all the ladies of Mount Olive Baptist Church would gather around me, fussing like a cluck of chickens. "Oh child, yo' head sho' do look good," gushed one elder of the church. "Did yo' mama do that?"

"You know she did. Her mama always be keepin' her nice-lookin'," chimed in the first lady of the church. "Ev'ry Sunday, Sister Gault have her lookin' like a doll."

I blushed, but never said a word. I stood dutifully still and basked in their praises, secretly thanking my mama for making me feel beautiful—even when I ended up with a million pony-tails, so wild they looked like a bunch of spiders were having a meeting on my head.

VENUS DE MILO GAULT was born and raised in Cincinnati, Ohio. Currently a middle school education major at Northern Kentucky University, she is also the mother of one daughter, Jasmine Brianna, who would agree that her mother is a much better hairdresser than her grandmother.

Love's Code

ERIN LANE BEAM

As a child, I longed to be as close as possible to my mother, often lodging myself tight against her tiny body. Terrified that she would die, I imagined freak accidents in the grocery store parking lot. A stray cart (discarded by one of those nasty people who weren't taught any better by their own mothers) would slowly roll down the pavement, gaining momentum just before gruesomely pinning my mother to the minivan's bumper.

I imagined it my duty to protect my mother from rolling carts—and other unforeseen dangers. Often I was afraid to let her leave the house alone, convinced something terrible would certainly happen during the one errand I had foolishly decided to opt out of to hold yet another Barbie pageant in my basement.

My mother never laughed at my melodrama. Instead, she would rock me gently as she sang one of her original lullabies that consisted of a call and answer. When I was too frightened to answer, she sang both parts until I was ready to join in.

One day, we were in our usual position, me snuggled deep against her chest, rubbing my hands lightly over the words "Simply the Best Mom" on her Ace Hardware sweatshirt as she wrapped her arms around me, sprinkling my forehead with "angel kisses." Like usual, I whimpered and said, "Please don't leave me, Mommy."

"I'm not going anywhere," she said, winking. "But someday you will grow up and leave me."

"No . . . no I won't. I'll stay with you always. I'll even marry you when I grow up." I wanted to be her baby forever.

She laughed gently. "I love you, Miss E."

I abruptly sat up. "I love you is not enough, Mommy." I wailed, grabbing her face with my small hands. "We need more . . . a word just for us that really means I love you, but doesn't get worn out. We'll only say it when we really mean it so we don't use it up. And it will keep us safe always." The words rushed out so quickly I was out of breath.

"That's a great idea, Miss E., but what would that word be?" Her pupils dilated behind her hexagonal glasses.

I began making sounds, stretching out syllables to a non-sensical level. Together, we unleashed our imaginations and our tongues.

"Mooooseeeeaaa."

"Lakatiiiilllla."

"Beyaaaaannnnaaaa."

My mother playfully dropped to her knees. I dropped down to face her and continued issuing sounds, seeking one to capture our special bond.

"Hoolllmaaa" bubbled up out of my throat, and we immediately fell back laughing. "How about hoolmaa, mommy . . . or holma. Doesn't that sound good?"

My mother squealed. "I love it. It sounds like holy, as in Holy Mary, Holy Mother, or hold me. I like the sound of it, Miss E. It's us. That's the word, then."

We now had a code word that would always bind us together and always keep us safe. I leaned back onto her, my stomach placid.

"Holma, mommy."

"Holma, Erin."

"Holma infinity."

"That's cheating, Erin."

If a shopping cart smashed her, at least I would know exactly what to put on her tombstone.

* * *

Years later, I was curled up in a shower stall, staring at the green tile of my freshman dormitory bathroom. Even though my ear hurt from being pressed hard against the portable phone, I sat motionless, afraid to move.

"Honey, feeling homesick is completely normal," my mom said softly. She had already listened to muffled sobs for an hour. "Let me tell you something that will cheer you up . . ."

"No, it's not normal, Mom." I wanted to halt yet another pep talk. "You *have* to say that. Why do I have to like you as much as I do? *Nobody* thinks that's normal."

"Okay so you love your mother, and you're a little homesick. That's not so bad. You'll be fine as soon as you settle in."

I groaned and rubbed my sore earlobe.

"Well, can I tell you something, Miss E.?"

"If you must." I wiped my eyes and sat up, preparing for one of my mother's heartfelt but annoying stories. I needed comfort, to know that my mother was safe and missed me as much as I missed her. I did not need an inane story to cheer up.

"You're gonna love this," she said, her normal enthusiasm swelling. "Last night, one of my patients, an Indian mother who had just given birth, wasn't sure what to name her baby girl."

I sighed again, but my mother's voice sounded so determined and purposeful, I started listening—really listening rather than half-listening.

"Anyway, she began rattling off possible baby names for her new daughter, asking me to repeat them how an American would pronounce them, because you know, people are always saying foreign names wrong. But in all fairness, there *are* some weird baby names out there nowadays. Would you believe two wacky parents named their baby Candy the other day? And their last name was Cane . . . I'm not kidding, Erin."

"Mom!" I shouted, half angry at her rampant tangent and half laughing at the fate of baby Candy Cane.

"But this is a good story, Erin, listen. This darling Indian woman was running through her list of names, saying Jagrati, Janaki, Joyoti, Jilpa, you know. To me, they sounded ethereal, like the word we created years ago. So I told her that you and I had once made up a word to mean I love you in a special way, in a way only a mother and daughter can love each other. We say Holma."

My eyes were beginning to dry.

She continued, with drawn breath "When I said 'Holma,' I'm telling you her eyes lit up. And here's the best part . . . she said 'Ah yes, Holma. We have that word in our language.' And you know what it means, Miss E.?"

I stood to my feet. "Are you kidding, Mom? You're making this up. Aren't you?"

She paused for dramatic emphasis. "No, absolutely not. Don't you want to know what it means—really means?"

"Um, yeah."

"Higher than the heavens, more than words can express."

Goosebumps ran up my arms, and a warm rush of energy flushed through my body, settling into my bones. "Really?"

"Really. Isn't that amazing? Our word is bigger than either of us could have known."

I peered into the mirror and smoothed my dampened hair.

My mother's voice was soft again. "So goodnight, honey and . . . holma."

"Holma, Mommy."

"Holma infinity."

"Mommy, that's cheating."

ERIN LANE BEAM is a freelance writer and speaker on the intersection of faith and feminism. With a degree in anthropology and gender studies from Davidson College, she hopes to pursue a career in publishing. She and her husband, Rush, adopted an adorable mutt named Amelia.

Lucille's Beauty Salon

KAY WHITE BISHOP

During Oklahoma City's biggest real estate boom in 1957, my mother divorced my daddy, bought a red Chevrolet, and headed west for the big City. After searching for the perfect homestead, Mother staked her claim on three bedrooms, one bath, and one car in the suburbs. To "keep the wolf away from the door," Mom had Grandpa turn our new attached garage into Lucille's Beauty Salon.

"Your grandpa rode on the back of his daddy's horse in the Land Run in 1889," Mother bragged. "And my grandmother rode side saddle all over Potawatomie County asking, 'Methodist, Baptist, or Presbyterian?' to each Boomer. She tallied up her figures and up went the Baptist Church. Your grandma raised us four kids, and Grandpa ran our farm. The Dust Bowl nearly killed us. Grandma canned, quilted, cooked, and cleaned house from daylight to dark, and I helped. So you see girls, we are worker bees, and I am going to beautify the city one head of hair at a time. And you are my assistants."

While few mommies on our block even knew how to drive, our fancy mother owned her very own business and sped around in her Chevy. We occupied the backseat, where we donned sunglasses with rhinestone temples and chewed Beech-Nut. Being five years older, I naturally corrected my little sister Sherry's gum smacking and told her what to expect from her first day of kindergarten.

At the Sooner Beauty Supply, Mother bought Aqua Net, Zotos perms, henna rinses, and small tubes of Triple Lanolin hand lotion. Before she ordered 1,000 personal business cards with her last six dollars, I checked her spelling. Because we'd staked our claim near Buchanan Elementary School, I mounted my Flyer bicycle daily in my Brownies uniform and spent my afternoons selling Girl Scouts cookies and announcing Mother's intention.

"Oh, a divorce tragedy," said Mrs. Hock, our next-door neighbor "Poor little thing. I'll ask my husband for the money and see if he'll let me come to your mommy's salon. How old are you, dear?"

"I'm ten, and I buy savings bonds at Buchanan Elementary each week so I won't be caught flat broke when I grow up. Ma'am, there is no risk involved in beautification. And, the first hairdo is complimentary."

"Free?"

"Absolutely. My mother is a trained professional with a framed diploma signed by June Morkes, the inspector from the

State Board of Cosmetology. Ask for Lucille when you call Windsor 2-9047. Satisfaction guaranteed. How many boxes of cookies would you like today?"

Weekly Mother orchestrated dozens of ladies masterfully from the shampoo corner to the hydraulic chair to the hair dryer where they could also get a manicure. Mrs. Brown, a tiny Baptist, left Lucille's sporting a slightly teased brunette bubble with bangs. Mrs. Johnson, a smart, exhausted nurse with a lazy husband, had her tips frosted and looked ten years younger. When Mrs. Young, a blind diabetic, tapped her way to our door, mother created a stunning beehive for her that prompted our first personal congratulatory phone call from a husband.

Always ahead of the trends, Mother regularly attended classes and studied piles of *Photoplay* magazines. If Elizabeth Taylor's dark hair curled up, I got a perm. If Sandra Dee wore a platinum ponytail, Sherry's hair went upward. And, when Debbie Reynolds brushed her bangs backward with a clip, so did my mother and everyone else on our block.

From the corner of my mother's salon I learned that there is no love like your first. I also saw an appendix scar and learned to count change and make a bank deposit. My mother obeyed the laws of the State Department of Cosmetology almost more than the Holy Bible, and when I stood on a stool to put a little dye on her roots, it was always behind locked doors to avoid a run in with the law. All the problems of the world that passed through Lucille's Beauty Salon came out bearable in under an hour.

We three celebrated each successful week of the beauty business boom by going to Dairy Queen for a dipped cone with our terrier Dicky. Later we watched *The Lawrence Welk Show* or wrestling, starring former Olympian Danny Hodge because my mother believed a victory won after a hard fight was the only way to go.

Monday was typically the national day of rest for a beautician, but our mother spent the day sanitizing our entire shop and cleaning house while Sherry and I subtracted, punctuated, and square danced at school. To keep the wolf away from my door, I planned a career as a teacher or airline stewardess. Sherry set her sights on ballet or horse training.

My mother never held God responsible when the downturn of the financial market of Oklahoma City in 1960 changed everything. She never resented her customers when they came by to tell us they simply had to save their hairdo money for food. Some of the ladies even got jobs.

"It's just bad luck," mother said optimistically. "I'm going to get another job or two. A little hard work never hurt anybody. The wolf won't get through our door."

We girls said that we agreed.

When she took a job in someone else's salon across town, where the rich ladies lived, everything changed. I quit the Brownies and baton lessons and shuffled home from school with Sherry in tow. I helped her with multiplication tables while watching *The Mickey Mouse Club*. Dinner happened long after dark. No one said so, but we three ached for the three-ring circus and all its performers who had once occupied our little garage.

Mother moved from job to job for the next decade. While Sherry and I searched for government loans for college, I balanced

Mother's checkbook, and Sherry rubbed her aching feet. When our shiny car had deteriorated and barely ran anymore, a police wrecker mistakenly towed it away from the curb. We managed to laugh hysterically when we did the math and decided to buy a new one rather then pay the $50 towing fee.

Mother lived up to her pioneer heritage and eventually started a new home-based day care business where she worked twenty-four hours a day. She sometimes missed the salon business and grumbled that hair had gone downhill ever since Farrah Fawcett. "Women were not meant to blow dry their own hair," she'd say.

Sherry and I graduated from college and built careers, but—like our mother—we had to reinvent ourselves many times. Luckily, we had also embraced her favorite Sooner State motto "Labor conquers all things." If one of us ever got bored or took a breather, the other would channel Mother.

"Only boring people are bored. Take the Windex to that storm door, and make sure the wolf isn't on the porch."

KAY WHITE BISHOP, MEd, conducts creativity workshops for teachers, students, churches, and hospitals for the Oklahoma Writing Project. For more than twenty years, her humor has been published in books, literary and teen magazines, and newspapers, which keeps you-know-who away from the door. Kay, who still craves the scent of nail polish remover, won her first short story slam, has pioneered into standup comedy, and has no clue how to operate her new blog on *www.letslightenup.blogspot.com*.

The Retail Queen of Fairfield, Connecticut

ROBERT F. WALSH

The day after Thanksgiving, the masses descended upon the local retail outlets like water from a burst dam, flowing like lemmings through the aisles in a pre-Christmas frenzy. Janet Walsh, however, did not go to shop. She waited patiently at the Returns counter with a turkey, or at least what was left of it after her husband and seven kids had attacked it twelve hours earlier. The skeletal remains were easy to slip into the small plastic bag. Even the wishbone had long since been taken out and snapped. When the clerk arrived, the retail queen of Fairfield, Connecticut, slid the bag and her receipt across the counter. "It went bad," she said.

My mom understood the craftiness one must adopt when trying to feed a family of nine. She packed the family checkbook like a musket with coupons skinned from local newspapers. Trips to the grocery store equated to military operations as seven kids invaded the unsuspecting stores offering samples in the aisles on

Saturday afternoons. Who needed lunch when you could wolf down eight tiny slices of pepperoni pizza and wash it down with thimblefuls of the newest Coke product? Our family did not merely buy in bulk; we stocked up as if winter was coming to Valley Forge. Each grocery trip concluded with a game of culinary Tetris—employing surgical precision to wedge food into three separate freezers and two refrigerators. There was no rummaging through the fridge in my family; when asked what was for dinner that night, my mom always answered, "Whatever's up front."

It was not uncommon for a loaf of bread to lie frozen in state—like Vladimir Lenin—for up to a year before being unearthed in the back of the freezer. When it made it to the front, Mom would thaw it like a wooly mammoth on those *National Geographic* specials, using a hair dryer to separate a few pieces for school lunches. These clay pigeons with peanut butter and jelly slathered all over them sat in our pails like a muttered apology, and were eaten, still frozen, when class had lunch. "It keeps the sandwich fresh," she'd say.

My mother also viewed the freezer as a time machine, cryogenically preserving batteries, cheeses, various cold medicines, and milk that would make the folks at Guinness or Ripley's take notice. In fact, there were three types of milk in our refrigerator: the "good" milk (within a week of its expiration date), "mixing" milk (older, used on cereal or in recipes), and "sour" milk (so designated when something inside it tried to bite you). "That expiration date is only a suggestion," my mom would say whenever we complained. "They just put it on there to make you buy more."

The retail queen also charmed local shopkeepers into 10 percent discounts for the privilege of clothing her family. "I have a carload full of customers in this family, growing children who like to buy new clothes!" She would say this, step back, smile, and then sweep her arm from child one to child seven, showing off her brood. The shopkeepers never realized that my innocent-looking mother put clothes into a rotation that would be the envy of the New York Yankees. You could pick a Walsh kid out of a crowd because my mom sewed massive patches on the insides of our pants and shirts resulting in an awkward Frankenstein gait. "You just have to work pants in a bit, like a baseball mitt," she'd say.

Each outfit bought for my oldest brother and sister filtered its way down to the youngest in a kind of corduroy waterfall. Our class pictures looked as if we'd just pasted a new head on last year's set. I was always ten years behind, trapped wearing a Fonzie T-shirt in a sea of Gap mock turtlenecks. As we grew older and more conscious of our fashion maladies, Mom tried to assuage our pain by buying toddler-sized, used Izod shirts, snipping off the logos, and sewing them onto Wal-Mart shirts. "That's strange," my friends would say, "I always thought the alligator was on the other side!"

Growing up with my mom, one learned that opened bags of candy on store shelves were considered "samples," and that any expensive item mistakenly placed in a discount section had to be sold at the discounted price. Four-dollar wine became vintage when poured into a different bottle. Clothes could be "rented" from local stores for special occasions and returned the very next day as long as you pinned the tags to the inside sleeve and kept the crease. Armed with a receipt and the original bag, there was nothing you couldn't return.

My mom's ability to make the most out of little was impressive, but her ability to make her family feel loved far surpassed it. She never missed an opportunity to tell us how much she loved us, even when we'd given her little reason to feel that way, let alone declare it. Even though we had the audacity to complain that everyone else's mom bought them new ones, our mom constructed elaborate prom dresses and dozens of Halloween costumes from scratch. Long before carpooling, she chauffeured seven kids to tennis matches, swim practices, track meets, Ping-Pong clubs, soccer practices, and after school tutors. She made midnight calls to bedrooms to put cold washcloths on fevered heads and to rub stinky Vicks on stuffed-up chests. She came to every banquet, even when her child was only there to pick up a "Participant" ribbon.

I plan to thank my mom by showering my own children with love—and with whatever I can afford, and occasionally with what I cannot afford. Most important, I'll teach them about the way life can be enjoyed even when you don't have money. They'll laugh often because they'll grow up listening to a lifetime of stories around the kitchen table—many of them about the retail queen. They'll see that the affection you feel for your family always trumps possessions.

And if the need arises, they'll find me waiting in line at the grocery store Returns counter with a half-eaten holiday ham in the original bag, receipt in hand, wondering how the heck the retail queen of Fairfield, Connecticut, ever managed to keep her cool.

ROBERT F. WALSH writes in between the tides of his true passion: teaching. He lives with his wife and their two dogs in Connecticut. Mr. Walsh's work has been published in, among others, *Pindeldyboz*, *Eclectica Magazine*, and *Small Spiral Notebook*. His nonfiction is included in the books *In Our Own Words: A Generation Defining Itself* (Vol. 5) and *In Our Own Words: A Generation Defining Itself* (Vol. 6). Even as his publishing credits grow, he is most proud of the fact that he has taught one of his cocker spaniels to "heel" on command.

Love in a Time of War

PAUL M. BONNELL

In 1959, Pat Bonnell crossed North America by train, and then the Pacific Ocean on a merchant ship bound for Vietnam. She had studied nursing in New Orleans and linguistics in Arkansas and intended to serve as a linguist. When she arrived in Vietnam, however, she discovered a greater need in public health and immediately set to work building clinics, helping orphans and lepers, and providing basic health care for the refugees displaced by war.

For the next thirteen years, Pat lived with the Vietnamese and Montangard villagers in places whose names would come to have meaning for a whole generation of Americans: Kontum, Pleiku, Nha Trang, Da Nang, and Khe Sanh. Over the years, Pat learned to write *quoc ngu*. She learned to speak Bru. She survived on *pho*, the staple noodle soup of Vietnam, and French bread. Sometimes she wore the *ao dai*, the traditional silk dress and pants attire of

Vietnamese women, and sometimes seersucker, chosen occasionally to remind her of central Florida.

When war erupted, she endured the squeal and thump of mortar fire from her home near the demilitarized zone. She rode in *xichlos* (bicycle carts), maneuvered a beat-up Land Rover through muddied red clay, and flew in Bell Huey helicopters, the characteristic whup, whup, whup of their rotor blades creating rhythmic memories that lasted decades, beating themselves into her experiences and memories. She survived the Tet Offensive of 1968 and watched horrified as the ravages of war unfolded around her. but rather than recoil from her duties, she redoubled her efforts to help the people she had come to love.

In 1972, Pat lived in Ban Me Thuot, a city in the South Central Highlands, not far from Cambodia and the Ho Chi Minh Trail, the North Vietnamese Army's major conduit in their advance toward Saigon. On Christmas Day, Pat carefully packaged remnants of the Christmas dinner that she and her friends had shared and carried it to the local hospital for her friend Aring, who had just given birth to a girl. When Pat entered the maternity ward, a remarkably tall, elderly Vietnamese woman recognized her and approached her hesitantly.

"Ma'am," the woman said, a look of panic in her eyes. "We know that you have taken care of many babies. My grandson is in very poor health. Could you help him?"

"Yes, of course, whatever I can do," Pat answered softly. "Where is he?"

"He is here. He is two days old. His father was killed two weeks ago in the war," the child's grandmother explained. "His mother is very sick and has no breast milk. Could you help care for him?"

Indeed, the child's mother had toxemia, a resistant case of malaria, and was visibly distraught over the recent death of her husband. She was not able to care for her infant. Without immediate intervention, her frail, six-week premature son would die.

As they moved into an examining room and Pat gently touched the tiny, two-day-old infant, weighing in at less than five pounds, the baby seemed to smile.

"He's smiling at the death angels," the resident midwives said somberly.

With barely an inkling of the weight of the moment, Pat enfolded the two-kilogram precious bundle in her arms and vowed to do whatever she could to help him.

He had neither a sucking reflex, nor the strength to nurse from a bottle or breast so Pat found an eyedropper, filled it with formula, gently tilted the baby's head back so the liquid would not dribble out, and then fed him eyedropper by eyedropper. Within days, she was able to ask Aring if she would share her breast milk to save the boy's life. Because Aring was producing an abundance of milk, she happily fed him along with her daughter, Mual, who had been born the same day.

Day by day, the premature boy began to gain weight, and at his mother's urging, Pat took him into her own home to care for him. As his mother recovered, she occasionally visited the baby at Pat's home, but showed no signs of wanting to take him. She remained distraught about the death of her husband, plus she was grappling with the harsh realities of having an older child, and had neither the resources, nor the energy to take care of a sick baby. Pat happily agreed to continue nursing the baby to health. Young Bru women who lived with Pat watched the baby while Pat worked. Because the mother never selected a name, Pat asked if she could call him Paul, after a friend who had often prayed for the infant and supported Pat in her extra duties.

Sometime later, Paul's mother moved far away to find employment, once again leaving Paul in Pat's care, essentially "asking" her to raise the baby as her own. Although Pat had fallen in love with her Christmas surprise, without a husband or a partner at the time, Pat wondered if she was the right person to raise the child. Her friends, however, had no doubts. "He's already your son," they said in unison. "He has been all along."

When Pat traveled to Saigon to apply for adoption, she learned that the only way she could have him naturalized was to leave Vietnam. Reluctantly, with a sense of foreboding, Pat packed up her belongings and boarded a plane to Guam.

Two days later, the North Vietnamese Army won a decisive victory in a surprise attack on the ARVN forces in Ban Me Thuot. They captured the Americans and marched them toward Hanoi. Many of those who did not die along the way later died in prisoner-of-war camps. Stranded—with no hope of returning—as soon as the adoption was complete, Pat and her son boarded another plane for Buffalo, New York. As the story of American involvement in Vietnam came to an end, Pat also ended hers. For us, however, it also marked the end of the beginning, as my mother and I made our way safely home.

PAUL M. BONNELL now lives with his family in Idaho. He teaches high school and belongs to the Idaho Writers League. He hopes to return to Vietnam someday to visit his birthplace.

The Ballerina

CHERYL NAFZGAR

My grandmother probably saved my life. Maybe that's an exaggeration. Maybe she just kept me from becoming a homicidal maniac, or maybe she saved me from skidding off the road and crashing into the trees. In reality, no miraculous intervention occurred. Grammy saved me by simply loving me while my parents spent years ignoring their three kids and obliviously fighting their way to an ugly divorce.

We spent all holidays and most weekends at my mother's parents' house. From our home in Barstow, we followed Route 66 through the Mojave Desert and over Cajon Pass, into the San Bernardino Basin, where my grandparents lived. My brother, baby sister, and I would be lined up on the backseat of the Oldsmobile. In summer, we would all be wearing shorts, the backs of our legs sticking to the vinyl seat, our perspiring arms and legs bumping against each other every time the car hit a dip. All the windows and both wind wings would be open to take advantage of the evaporative cooling effect on our sweaty bodies. In winter, we would make the trips bundled in itchy wool sweaters with the car heater blazing, all of us nodding off to sleep in the backseat until my brother said he was carsick. Then we'd pull off the road so he could get out and throw up in the sage brush.

As soon as we reached our grandparents' house, the three of us would jump out of the backseat and run up the front steps and through the never-locked front door, each of us eager to be the first one to reach our grandmother.

Grammy would always emerge from the kitchen, wiping her hands on her apron. She'd reach for as much of the three of us as she could include in an embrace that smelled of Pillsbury flour and Chanel no. 5. Then she'd tell us she'd just finished filling the cookie jar, and we'd gather around the kitchen table, competing to be heard over Tommy Tucker, my grandfather's canary, singing from his cage in the corner.

Unlike anyone else in the family, Grammy was short, fat, and big bosomed. She predated women's liberation, so never learned to drive, and depended on either my grandfather or the bus for transportation. My grandfather gave her weekly spending money, and the only way she was able to get anything extra was to save Green Stamps. She would sit at the kitchen table, filling up the pages of her Green Stamp Book until she had enough to order something from the stamp catalog—almost always something for the kitchen.

If Grammy wasn't in the kitchen canning fruit for her cellar stockpile, crocheting an antimacassar, embroidering pillowcases, reading a book, or listening to piano music on the record player,

I could usually find her in her sewing room braiding rugs. Every Tuesday she took the bus to her braided-rug-making class, and she eventually covered the wooden floors of every room. The people who supplied the old clothes for her braided rugs might be long gone, but their woolen trousers would live forever, woven into her rug under the dining room table, soaking up the home-made applesauce I spilled.

Grammy was always busy, but she was never too busy for me, or any of her other grandchildren. On rainy days, she would turn us loose in the cellar and let us rummage through large steamer trunks filled with old shoes, clothes, top hats, beads, and toys. Or she would let us take turns cranking her old Victrola and listen to Rudy Vallee's reedy tenor voice crooning "As Time Goes By." She endured endless repetitions of "Chop Sticks" on her upright piano, patiently answered a stream of stupid questions, unlocked locked drawers and closets, and brought up boxes of old cards and beads from the cellar. Nothing was ever off limits.

To us, she was the consummate grandmother, but little did we know that she once had dreams of her own. A framed picture on my grandfather's bureau captured an image of Grammy as a youthful ballerina, wearing a skirt of netting that hugged her slender waist. This was not the grandmother I knew, the one who wore flowery cotton house dresses and kept her whalebone corset hanging on the back of the bathroom door.

Only much later did I learn that my grandmother had studied with a prestigious dance company in Boston at the turn of the century and dreamed of becoming a classical ballerina. She had even been offered the opportunity to join a professional troupe, but she had to decline when she developed asthma and then met my grandfather. The asthma depleted the breath she needed to dance, and my grandfather refocused her life on marriage and raising three daughters.

As she aged, my grandmother's body showed more than the usual signs of betrayal. Her arms and leg muscles weakened, her skin became so thin it barely concealed the bones beneath, and she bruised easily. One arm, broken in a fall and screwed back together, forever hung cattywompas in a sling. Eventually, she needed a portable oxygen tank, connected by tubes to her nose, to breathe. However, no matter how much her health declined, my grandmother always said she felt twenty-five.

My grandmother had a nightly exercise routine. Every night, before climbing into bed with my grandfather, she emptied a jar of marbles onto the floor next to the bed, picked them up one by one with her toes, and dropped them back into the jar. She learned this exercise when she was a dancer. It strengthened her feet, and especially her toes, for ballet dancing.

My grandmother's exercises kept her in touch with her dreams of becoming a ballerina, something she knew she was, somewhere deep inside her broken and old body.

CHERYL NAFZGAR is a retired book and magazine editor who grew up in the Mojave Desert in the 1950s and now lives in northern California. "The Ballerina" is a chapter in *Mojave Daughter*, a memoir she has written. She is currently writing a second book.

The Beti Weitzner Salon

JOAN LOGGHE

My mother once had the best beauty shop in Pittsburgh. She had dreamed of becoming a schoolteacher, but her family had lost so much money in the Great Depression she had to settle for beauty college. At least that's what she told me, but one never knew. My mother had a way of stretching the truth. She lied to get into kindergarten, and she lied about her age so she could get her first job when she was thirteen. She had even neglected to tell me that she was married before and that my brother had a different father.

Nevertheless, my mother was also a charmer who had the kind of charisma that lit up a room. Whatever she did, she did with flair and pizzazz, and so it was that she created the Beti Weitzner Salon and turned it into the hot beauty shop of its day. She kept her maiden name for business, not that it was her real and true name. Beti with an "i" in a Hungarian family was an anomaly—unless you gave birth to my mother's persona.

Her shop was on the second floor of the Carlton House Hotel in bustling downtown Pittsburgh, the swankiest place to be and so new we had watched it being built. You'd enter to find a uniformed doorman, ride a fancy elevator to the second floor, turn right, et voila!—the Beti Weitzner Salon. My mother went back to work when I was two weeks old and worked six days a week for forty years—in high heels. Luckily, she loved her work, soon supported twenty employees, and provided everything beauty—from facials to pedicures—to Pittsburgh's elite.

Even as a young girl, I loved being in the buzzing salon. Whenever I entered, I was greeted warmly and marched down the aisles to personally greet the customers, sitting under dryers, their foil-wrapped hair slathered with purple bleach. On weekends, I would answer the phone, take appointments, and help with inventory, and my mother loved showing me off. Even though I was often relegated to the task of removing bobby pins from pin curls that invariably stuck to the scalps of the fragile, elderly women, I happily did all this just to be near my glamorous mother in her glamorous salon.

My mother specialized in coloring hair and won trophies from New York that she proudly displayed in her salon. As long as I knew her, she wore her blonde hair upswept and looked so elegant I considered her my own Betty Grable, my movie star mother. As her notoriety spread, Revlon's owner Charles Revson and Fabergé's George Barrie became personal friends. She was even offered opportunities to work as a hair stylist in Hollywood, but she told us she didn't think it would be a good place to raise children. Truthfully, I think she preferred being a big fish in a small pond. In Pittsburgh, she was already a star. Everywhere we went, people greeted her as if she was celebrity.

Because Pittsburgh hosted pre-Broadway runs of plays in those days, my mother's salon attracted visiting celebrity customers. She soon lined their signed photos on the wall and often told me intimate stories about the likes of Patti Page, Ginger Rogers, Carol Channing, and Judy Garland. She once told me that Judy Holliday, when asked if she'd like to take off her dress and slip on a robe, rather than answer simply proceeded to strip in the middle of the aisle. "She didn't have a stitch on under her dress," my mother said, laughing.

My mother relished the outrageous. When Phyllis Diller became a frequent customer, my mother encouraged her to use flamboyant wigs for her show. Phyllis liked my mother so much that she redecorated the facial room, purchasing new furniture and an expensive chandelier to glam it up. Thereafter, my mother cheerfully ushered clients into the "Phyllis Diller Room" for facial pampering.

Oddly enough, my mother's one nemesis turned out to be fellow Hungarian Zsa Zsa Gabor. After my mother styled her hair, Zsa Zsa adopted an air and said, "But of course, Zsa Zsa never pays."

Not one to brook such nonsense, my mother kept her cool and then without missing an *old country* beat said, "At the Beti Weitzner Salon, Zsa Zsa pays."

When I was in high school, my mother brought Ginger Rogers home for dinner. They had become such close friends, my mother had fixed Ginger up with our handsome friend Paul, an oral surgeon, and they had had a fling. Heavily powdered, with extremely long nails, Ginger didn't particularly look like a movie star, but when she complimented my eyebrows and told me never to do a thing with them, I couldn't wait to tell my mother, who was forever trying to reform my hair, my outfits, and my friends.

My mother and I were, in fact, embroiled in a permanent makeover contest, and I was—unfortunately—always a prime *before* candidate. To her, I may have looked mousy, like a girl choosing to hide in the shadows. Or perhaps she just liked viewing me as a challenge. She had become an avid golfer who would exert great effort to win, at all costs.

Upon retirement, when my mother sold the Beti Weitzner Salon, the photos of the stars vanished, and the Carlton House Hotel was imploded to make room for the U.S. Steel Tower. Nevertheless, my mother remained glamorous and active. She cooked for the first time in her life, learned to play bridge, and won golf club championships well into her eighties.

At age eighty-nine, my mother inadvertently let her bleached hair go white and baby chick soft. One of my last, fondest memories came when a Cuban hairdresser named Julian came to her home with a cape and scissors to style her hair. As he worked his magic, my mother looked so blissful, lost in a trance, like a beatific saint. Not long after, she drifted into the light, where I like to imagine her—comb and scissors in hand—holding court in the ultimate beauty parlor.

JOAN LOGGHE surrendered her mother's suggestion of Joni with an "i" and went on to write poetry and teach as Joan. She happily sports white hair and has six books to her credit, plus a National Endowment for the Arts grant in poetry. She currently runs a collaborative press, *www .treschicasbooks.com.*

Sanctuary

PAVITHRA SRINIVASAN

"Well, she's a little coal baby, isn't she?" asked an aunt of mine. We were at a marriage reception, and all of my aunts wore voluminous silk saris and were dripping in gold and diamonds. Most of my relations were remarkably beautiful people—regal roman noses, sparkling eyes, luxuriant hair, and skin as soft as rose petals.

Amma, my mother, bristled at their remarks, but she did her best to hide it. "Considering that my husband and I are both dark-skinned, I'd be surprised if she looked like a snow maiden," she said dryly.

Among the predominantly dark-skinned Dravidian women of Southern Tamil Nadu, India, having fair skin was highly desirable, particularly for a girl. Fair-skinned babies were cuddled more often, and when a fair-skinned girl reached marriageable age, the best grooms waited in line and offered the highest price for them.

Not so for darker-skinned girls—and my relations made it very clear with their veiled remarks that they pitied me.

Because I heard this often, I shied away from people. I detested social events where my fair-skinned cousins ultimately surrounded me, making me the cynosure of all eyes. I cringed in embarrassment when my own aunts and uncles narrowed their eyes when they saw my dark form moving among their lighter selves.

"You little idiot," Amma said, when she found me crying. "Yes, your skin is dark. All the creams and lotions in the world won't change your skin color, but why would you want it to?"

"Because my cousins are my grandparents' favorites. Other than you and *Appa* (my father), no one ever hugs me or even touches me," I said, sniffling.

As if to avoid crying herself, Amma bit her lip, sat down, and then combed her fingers through my hair. "You'll probably never believe this, but you *are* beautiful, and I'm not just seeing you through a mother's eyes. You inherited my brains and my love for the arts. You have something tangible that they don't. Make sure you use your gifts."

Because I loved writing and showed some affinity for it, Amma bought me reams of paper and pencils "so you can write your first novel." Everyone in the family thought we were being foolish and made derisive remarks. Amma always grew angry. "Never mind who laughs at you," she insisted. "You must take up this challenge. You must work hard and become a writer."

One evening, as I was changing my uniform from school, Amma came to my room and stood at the door hesitantly. "I wanted to tell you this before you heard it elsewhere," she began. "We've lost all our money. Your father has been speculating in the stock market, and it's all gone." Over the course of the next year, my parents had to sell their businesses, as well as our two houses in the city. Eventually we lost everything, including the car.

Because we couldn't afford rent anywhere else, we moved into my grandmother's home. Amma's face often looked grim at night, so I would scramble from my mat and sit with her, holding her hand. My mother had also signed all the loan documents along with my father, and prison loomed as a very distinct possibility. I worried about her all the time.

"I'm not going to kill myself, my girl," Amma would say, gazing at the fan that rotated slowly from the ceiling. "That would be cowardly, and it would leave you stranded. I will not leave you stranded."

Both of my parents worked several jobs. Amma left at seven in the morning and did not return until 8 P.M. I would greet her and immediately begin chattering about my day, trying to cheer her up. She was clearly exhausted, but she always made time to listen to me, sitting patiently with me for hours as I talked about my writing.

"It's good that you write," Amma said one evening. "But why aren't you writing stories? You always liked fiction. Why not start writing fiction for magazines?"

"I don't know how to write fiction," I said. "I'm afraid anything I wrote would be bad, a waste of effort."

Amma would wave her hand as if to brush the thought out of the air. "You've got nothing to lose. Look at us. Your father and I were left with nothing, but we are coming back. It's the same for you. Let me have the happiness of seeing you look cheerful, my girl."

Once, I asked her why she was so keen that I write. It wasn't normal for a middle-class Chennai housewife to support her daughter in this way. Most women did not want a career; they were usually content with marriage and children.

"I want you to have something for yourself," Amma said. "Then, if the world shuts you out, or if people jeer at you, you will have a place where you can restore yourself. Writing provides a sanctuary. It gives you a respite before you have to meet the world again. I'm hoping writing will give you what I didn't have."

When my first short story was published, Amma held it in her hands for a long time, as if in a trance. Finally, she said simply, "When's the next coming out?"

These days, my relatives no longer feel sorry for me, nor do they make any veiled or openly rude comments about my dark skin. They now proudly refer to me as "the writer" and show their respect by asking my opinion about the latest developments in the publishing world.

I have had many stories published, but Amma still carefully cuts out each article or story as soon as it appears and places it in a portfolio. She spends many hours cataloging my work and preparing Excel files to keep track of it. "It takes my mind off my troubles," she explains. But when I occasionally stumble upon her leafing through the files, rereading each published piece,

I know that that it means a great deal more to her than something to do.

Occasionally, when I catch her almost literally caressing the pages, I ask her if she is being sentimental, but she always shakes her head as if I am being silly and always asks the same thing. "When's the next coming out?"

PAVITHRA SRINIVASAN is a freelance author, translator, and editor. Getting published remains an uphill task, but she still sticks with it. When the world turns its back on her, the door to her writing sanctuary is always open.

The Rolling File Cabinet

RUTH ANDREW

D riving down Cervantes Street with my mother one day in Pensacola, Florida, in our family's green Plymouth, we heard something go clunk. Then another clunk and another and another followed. In the 1950s, many housewives would have relied on their husbands to deal with car troubles, but my mother always thought for herself. She knew exactly what to do. She quickly pulled into her favorite service station.

"Something's wrong with my car," she informed the mechanic.

"Nice to see you, Mrs. Parks." All the service station attendants knew my mother by name—even though 80,000 people populated Pensacola at the time. My mother described the problem. "I'll take a look at her for you," he replied, smiling. In 1959, mechanics could still be found at virtually every gas station, fixing engine trouble and changing tires.

After probing and prodding for about twenty minutes, the mechanic looked up at Mother with dubious eyes, a frown on his face, and a wrinkled brow. "Well, I'm sorry to have to tell you this, Mrs. Parks, but you've got a serious problem here. Now we can order the parts and get this fixed, but it's going to be expensive. Unless you have the original warranty on your car, I don't think we can give you a break on the price."

My mother then frowned, but her eyes quickly twinkled again. "You mean if I have the original paperwork, you can fix whatever is wrong with it and not have to charge me anything?"

"Yes, that's right, Mrs. Parks, but this car is pretty old. You and Mr. Parks must have bought it at least ten years ago, and not many people keep all the receipts. We would need the original receipt and paperwork, receipts for repairs, and so on." He stressed the word "original."

My mother, not any taller than the top of the car, stepped back and clicked her fingers as if she'd suddenly had a brilliant idea. "Just let me have a look in the trunk," she said brightly.

"The trunk?"

"Yes. That's where I keep my paperwork." Mother said this as if this was normal, as if she were a secretary accessing her file cabinet in a sunny plush office.

The mechanic and I stepped aside and watched as mother unlocked the trunk and dove so deeply into it her top half disappeared into the back end of the Plymouth. She quickly retrieved a shoebox stashed in the corner of the trunk and thumbed through a box packed full of receipts. Within two minutes, donning a smile, she waved a yellowed piece of paper, a pink carbon page flapping behind it.

Although slightly flushed, my mother's face beamed. "Is this what I need?"

The mechanic leaned forward and gazed in amazement at the piece of paper. It *was* the original receipt, exactly what he needed. Seconds later, she pulled out all of the original paperwork for the car—the original contract agreements, the warranty, as well as receipts for every single, teeny-tiny repair ever done to our family's Plymouth. We would have to wait days for them to acquire the parts for the car, but my mother forked over those papers in a snap.

So we drove home, enduring the clunks in the way one can do when one knows the problem has been solved, parked the ailing car under the carport, and waited three days for the call from the station announcing that the parts had arrived. Two days later, my mother drove the fully repaired car home, and it didn't cost her a dime.

To this day she keeps every receipt that crosses her palm. If she has a fan belt repaired for her car, even though I've told her often she doesn't need to hold onto that kind of receipt, she keeps it anyway. If she has a windowpane repaired in her house, she feels compelled to file the receipt in her "household repairs" folder. If the heating repairman comes out to change the filter, the receipt for service is tucked into the folder.

Being my mother's daughter, I also cling to paperwork, and in an office setting, I totally get the concept of filing cabinets and making sure paperwork is filed away properly, but at home, I'm disorganized. At most I scrawl a year on a white envelope and then cram whatever warranties I acquire that year into it, or I shove car repair receipts into a drawer along with a jumble of receipts dating back seven years. In reality, I'm paperwork challenged, and all my friends know it. Trust me—there's no magic shoebox in my trunk.

Thus I was all the more delighted when a former boss recently told a friend how much he missed having me work for him. "Ruth always knew right where everything was and could put her finger on a file at a moment's notice."

"I get that from my mother," I told my friend, beaming.

RUTH ANDREW is a freelance writer living in Spokane, Washington. Her previous short stories and humor articles have appeared in many newspapers and lifestyle magazines. You can read more about her at *www .iecrwa.com/bios/ruthandrew.html*.

From Mumsey, with Love

JULIE ANDERSON

All my life, I've heard how much my mother loves me. Not from my mother—although I've heard this from her often—but from virtual strangers: neighbors, landlords, and mailmen. A month after my arrival in college, the mailroom clerk, handing me my tenth package, smiled and said brightly, "Your mother sure loves you a lot."

Then, when I went to Rome two years later, Pasquale Pesce, the director of my study abroad program, informed me in his lilting Italian accent that I was very, very lucky to have a mama who sent me all those boxes and letters. I had better appreciate all she did for me, he said, wagging a finger.

Twenty years later, I try not to laugh when people tell me this. How can I explain that I've heard it so often, from the oddest people, that it has almost become a joke? Not that I'm not grateful. I am. To be loved as deeply as my mother loves me—well, there's nothing like it in the world.

My mother was born in London on the day Hitler invaded Poland. One year later, during the German blitz, my mother, along with all children under the age of fifteen, was evacuated from the city. In my mother's case, however, the plan to keep her safe in the English countryside failed miserably. She wailed nonstop for her mother until the family who had taken her in brought her back to London, delivered her into my grandmother's arms, and then literally ran from the house, vanishing down the street before my grandmother had a chance to object. But my grandmother was secretly glad; she adored my mother and had suffered just as much from the separation. Some time later, my mother ran down a street of sooty row houses and saw a smoking pit where a friend's home had stood only the night before.

In 1964, one week before the Beatles landed, kicking off the British Invasion, my mother arrived in New York City on a freighter that cost her fifty pounds—two-thirds of her life savings. I can picture her, age twenty-four, walking down the plank in her baby-blue mini-dress, matching purse and heels, her fashionably cropped hair, frosted lipstick, and blue eyeshadow. She would have stopped, put down her little plastic suitcase, flipped open her compact, checked her hair and makeup, and then gazed around her at the city she was determined to make her new home. The new city looked shockingly tall and different: London did not have New York's towering modern chic, glass and concrete skyscrapers, big new cars, and fast, brightly lit roads. She fell in love with it immediately. She was sick of her native city's gray weather, its old, dusty buildings, its propriety and politeness.

She was tired, too, of being judged by her working class accent and her lack of education. Just because she had to drop out of school at sixteen to earn money for the family didn't mean she was stupid. She had won scholarships and was always the "top girl" in her class. One day, therefore, en route to her job as a clerk at the Metal Box Company, she had said to herself, "Screw it, I'm leaving," and caught the next boat out of London. She would have preferred Australia. She liked Australian men with their rough exteriors and raucous humor, but the boat for Australia had already left, and she didn't want to wait another month for the next one.

Leaving was in her blood. My grandmother left Manchester for London when she was only eighteen, relying solely on her good looks and wits to find work in the big city. Before that, my grandmother had come to England from Ireland, again alone and looking for a better life. My mother made her own way to America, and it was only a matter of time before my turn came. After college, when I ventured as far as China, the family joked that I moved so far west I ended up in the Far East. In the ensuing years, I moved often, until I eventually settled in San Francisco, slightly closer to my mother.

Wherever I went, my mother never stopped sending me letters and packages, perhaps precisely because she knew well the value of mail. When trans-Atlantic phone calls were unspeakably expensive, she kept up an avid correspondence with her mother. And even though we now live in an age where we can talk on the phone for only a few cents a minute or e-mail for free, there's nothing quite like finding my mother's envelopes and boxes on my doorstep.

It's not simply because I like the clippings and chocolates, the reviews and lipsticks, the photographs and earrings my mother sends. It's because of what they imply. These envelopes and boxes not only imply love, as many have noted, but permission, a tacit approval of my going off to find my own new place. Though it must have been unspeakably hard—as it was for my grandmother and great-grandmother—my mother sent me off into the world with immeasurable generosity and goodwill, relinquishing that which she loved best. I can't think of a more heroic gesture than that.

JULIE ANDERSON lives in Berkeley, California. She has recently been published in the *Gettysburg Review*, *Other Voices* (Canada), and *Teacher Miracles*, an anthology of stories about teaching. Her mother's most recent package to her included photographs, an electric blue scarf, and a book called *French for Cats*.

Matka, the Little Polish Dynamo

JAMES A. SCHIELDGE

"Hold still!" My mother held my chin firmly in one hand, spat onto the wadded handkerchief, and rubbed my dirty face. I didn't like it. What little boy would? First, it hurt. Second, we were in public, and I was sure the whole world was watching. I stood still and stared at her brow, scrunched up in concentrated effort. You didn't argue with Mom.

One of three children born of Polish immigrants, my mother, Henrietta Uliasz, felt the sting of discrimination inside, as well as outside, the family. Yankee bluebloods looked down on their Slavic neighbors in their gentrified Connecticut town. To them, speaking in broken English and cooking strange foods like kielbasa and pierogies represented an inferior class of people. When my mother was a little girl, the town council approved the creation of a public dump and designated the Polish section for its location. The day they put up the sign across the street from her house, my grandmother grabbed my mother's hand and marched to city hall. By the time her mother finished lambasting them, the town fathers relented and cancelled the order, and my mother learned how to stand up for herself.

When my grandfather died, my grandmother remarried and bore three more children. The new father showered attention on his own offspring but relegated his stepchildren to second-class status. My mother was sent off to work while her half-brothers and half-sister were encouraged to continue their educations. My mother suffered many slights and verbal abuse. When she came home one evening, her stepfather called her a foul name and demanded that she hand over her meager earnings.

Something in her snapped. She straightened her back, drew up all of her five-foot-two-inch frame and stepped up to his towering figure. "I'm not giving you a penny, you S.O.B," she shouted. "And don't you ever call me that name again. Do you understand me?"

Her stepfather raised his hand to slap her, but froze when he saw my mother's fierce resolve. Slowly, he lowered his hand. "Tak," he said simply. "Yes." He never bothered her again.

Despite the abuse she suffered, Mom personified the word charismatic. Quick to laugh and friendly to all, people clustered around her just to enjoy her company. Combined with charisma, her skill and intelligence distinguished her in the workplace, as well. At the urging of her supervisor, she entered a typing contest and easily blew away the competition, typing a sizzling speed of 150 words per minute on a manual typewriter. Her mind was as quick as her fingers, and she quickly progressed up the ladder at the insurance company until she married and left to raise a family.

My father delivered mail in East Hartford, but he always had grand moneymaking plans to put us on Easy Street. One involved chicken farming. He read a book, bought some chickens, and fenced off the backyard. Mom would stand at the window, watching hens and chicks running everywhere, frowning. Gamely, she went door to door selling the eggs to the neighbors, but it soon proved a disaster. Mom's gregarious personality worked against her. She would stop at a house, sell a couple of eggs, and then chat with the neighbor for an hour. Eventually, the chickens far outnumbered egg sales. When the chicken population got out of hand, Dad housed them in the attic, where we could hear them running around clucking and fighting all night. "Either the chickens go, or I go," Mom told Dad. One look at her, and the era of chicken farming came to an end.

When Dad had endured one New England blizzard too many as a mail carrier, he migrated to California, and then sent for us. World War II was raging, and trains were filled with military personnel. A young and friendly mother traveling with three little children, without her husband, made an attractive target for a lonely serviceman. One sailor struck up a conversation with Mom and invited us all to his compartment. Soon after, he sent the three of us to get ice cream. Minutes later, we saw Mom, tromping down the aisle, looking furious. We never saw the sailor again, but I suspected he would have preferred facing a South Seas typhoon to the Polish storm he had surely encountered.

Once settled in California, Mom worked full-time while continuing to do a hands-on job of raising her children. The Polish word for mother is *matka*, which—in my case—could have been an acronym for "Mom Always Treated Kids with Affection." She was also the head of the house. She handled the finances, planned the social calendar, acted as a Cub Scouts den mother, and was actively involved in all our school activities. She insisted that we attend parochial school and would sit us down and give us an old-fashioned scolding when we transgressed, so much so *matka* could also have been an acronym for "Mom At-no-time Tolerates Kids' Antics."

Mom soon rose to personal secretary for a prominent commercial building contractor, joined the national organization Women in Construction, and became its president. She even received a certificate of achievement from then Los Angeles mayor Sam Yorty, who called her "a remarkable woman."

Still disappointed that she had been denied an education, Mom insisted all three of her kids attend college. My brother earned a doctorate and enjoyed a long career with NASA's Jet Propulsion Laboratory. My sister worked as an accountant for Los Angeles County's Department of Health Services. I entered the fire service, rose to the rank of battalion chief, and later taught fire technology at the local college. We all wanted Mom to be proud of us and wanted to show her how much we appreciated her many sacrifices in raising us.

Once, after a large fire where I served as Incident Commander and directed operations that were broadcast on the television news, I stopped by Mom's home to tell her all about it, my face smeared with soot. She sat listening for a minute, then pulled out her wadded handkerchief, spat on it, and took my chin. "Hold still," she ordered. I sighed. Some things never change.

JAMES A. SCHIELDGE retired after thirty years as a firefighter. He is currently working on two books, a novel drawing on his many experiences as a firefighter and a how-to book for candidates wishing to enter the fire service. He loves cooking the wonderful Polish dishes his matka taught him to make.

The Princess Who
Reinvented Herself

JEAN GANT

Turning fifty, I took the "now or never" plunge to call my long-lost father in New Jersey. My stepmother, Mori, answered, "He doesn't handle surprises well. Let me talk to him when he gets home. Call back tomorrow."

That Thanksgiving, after forty-three years of no contact, I flew from Seattle for a catchup weekend. Mori danced around us as Daddy and I stumbled over each other's questions. She carefully planned every meal and outing. At seventy-eight, she was bent over with scoliosis and walked with a cane. She pulled her white hair back in a ponytail and apologized that she had to go to Manhattan for a poetry workshop and a jazz concert. Dressed in colorful clothes with bold patterns, she insisted that I push her up the bus steps to go into the City alone, and sent us off to a movie and dinner "to get to know each other."

"Has she always been like this?" I asked my father. My own mother was a quiet southern lady. "No," he replied. "She used to be like other people, but about fifteen years ago she woke up one morning acting like it was the only day in her life, and she's been like that ever since."

Mori had studied architecture and visual arts at Pratt Institute and Fontainebleau. She worked as a draftsman in Manhattan and traveled alone in Europe, until at age thirty-five she met my father and became a wife and mother. Their son, Paul, proved a musical prodigy and studied with be-bop jazz teacher Barry Harris in New York. When Paul died suddenly in his mid-twenties, Mori (then in her mid-sixties) signed on as a singer in Barry's chorus. She also began to write poetry and to participate in multimedia events in New York and New Jersey.

Before I left that Thanksgiving, Mori gave me a book titled *On Women Turning Fifty* and talked about places we could travel together. "Wait, I need some time to assimilate all this," my father said.

Unfortunately, my father died the following November, and I decided to visit Mori that Christmas for what I thought would amount to closure. My suitcase arrived three days late. Mori delighted in sharing her clothes, saying her mother had dressed her like a mannequin until she was twelve, so she had always wanted a daughter, to let her choose her own clothes. We talked deep into the nights, drinking tea and eating Clementine cookies. Stories of my father and the brother I never met filled a hunger from my childhood that nothing in my own rich, eventful life had ever touched.

Tentatively, Mori asked me if I'd like to go to a Solstice Celebration with her ritual group. "Not exactly a witch's coven," she explained. At dawn, we greeted the return of the light with a large circle of women in a cold and snowy backyard. Then, over oatmeal and hot tea, I met Mori's friends and fellow artists—women of all ages, talents, and backgrounds, for whom Mori was the inspiring and beloved crone. I began to realize that Mori was no ordinary stepmother.

Mori gave me a copy of her chapbook *The Princess Who Re-Invented Herself*. We went to writers' groups, where members read and critiqued their work. When it was her turn, Mori stood up and *performed* a short poem; all sat spellbound. She introduced me proudly as "my new-found stepdaughter." In her voice the words became an honored title. Maybe I had found a fairy stepmother?

We parted with plans to meet and travel. Mori visited Seattle and met my children and friends; she became family. Our relationship was never about her being an old woman without family. The magic of Mori's energy lit up every group she joined. Lives took on new significances in her presence.

We traveled to places neither of us had been. We met in Santa Fe, rented a car, and visited those who had left our communities for this strange land. When we met in Oak Park, Illinois, I had the double pleasure of discovering Frank Lloyd Wright buildings and seeing her delight as Mori the architect walked into them for the first time. We dreamed of further adventures—back to her beloved Switzerland, exploring unknown Iceland.

But Mori's life-long dream was to live in Manhattan. At eighty, she took on the task of moving out of her big yellow house in New Jersey. I visited her in August 2001, at her senior residence, four blocks from the World Trade Center. We reveled in the lovely community of Battery Park City. Mori was eager for September, when a Stuyvesant High School student would teach her how to use a computer and e-mail.

On 9/11, just as Mori glanced out her thirteenth-floor window as she headed downstairs for breakfast, the first plane hit the tower. Residents spent a day in the building basement with wet cloths covering noses and mouths to filter particles from the air, until a chartered bus took them to Yonkers, with only the clothes on their backs. When I found Mori and phoned several days later, I asked if any frail, elderly residents had suffered heart attacks or nervous breakdowns from this unthinkable experience. Mori laughed. "No, most of us have lived through two world wars; many lost family in the Holocaust. These things happen. But I'll never forget how the sunny morning suddenly went dark . . . ."

Mori stayed with friends in New Jersey for six weeks. The most difficult part of the experience, she told me, was having no ID, no way to prove who she was. She went back, of course, walking past Ground Zero every Thursday to work on her poetry at City College of New York's Quest Community for Lifelong Learning. Mori had a walker now, decorated by her ritual group with beads and ribbons. She used more taxis, fewer busses and subways.

I visited whenever I could, and Mori took me all over the City to museums, poetry readings, and jazz concerts. I met her jazz master, Barry Harris, and joined her at conferences for the International Women's Writers' Guild.

After several years and two bouts of pneumonia (from the "bad air" she had breathed in during 9/11), Mori moved uptown, then back to New Jersey. Shortly before her eighty-seventh birthday, Mori bundled up in her gray fur coat and had me push her up the bus steps to go to Manhattan to attend a contemporary ballet to watch my niece Jessica dance. When I introduced Mori, she had all the young ballerinas smiling as she declared, "Thank you! I'd forgotten how much I love the ballet. I dreamed of being a dancer when I was young."

Mori died a few weeks later, leaving a half-written poem on her coffee table. I found another scrawled on a band-aid box in the wastebasket. In her address book I discovered the password question Mori had used for her bank account: "Alive? Absolutely!"

JEAN GANT writes poetry, memoir, and nonfiction, and she is working on a book about her amazing blended family. She lives in Seattle, Washington, and works as an autism specialist and mental health therapist, specializing in Asperger's syndrome.

My Mietze

MONIKA KING, NARRATOR;
TAMMY L. GLASER, WRITER

My mother, Maria, pedaled her rickety bike to the train station, gasping for air, urging her legs to pedal faster. She longed to see my father before he boarded the train, longed for him to run his fingers through her golden curls, call her his Mietze ("Kitty"), and ask her to hug their three little girls. When she spied the taillights of his train leaving the station, her knees buckled.

The thought of her husband wielding a gun, instead of a violin, pierced her heart. Hitler had vowed to exempt educators from the draft, but now her Hans—a Berlin school superintendent fluent in four languages—had been forced to become an officer in the German army. Even though their insane dictator had promised unity with Stalin, Mietze's only love had been assigned to the first wave sent to invade Leningrad in 1941. Months later, an envelope bearing his wedding band and news of his senseless death arrived.

In 1943, we moved into a cramped apartment in East Prussia. Mama's brothers owned farms nearby in Germany's breadbasket, where she hoped to keep us fed and safe from the Allied bombing that had devastated Berlin. Nevertheless, we soon heard shrill sirens announcing bombers approaching Königsberg, and Mama herded us downstairs to the bomb shelter. We were told to go to another shelter across the street, underneath the garages. The four of us huddled in the darkness listening to the hum of the approaching planes and the soft whistle of dropping bombs. Mama remained calm, attempting to soothe our burgeoning fears as deafening explosions assaulted our ears and the ground trembled.

When the motorized noises dampened to a soft drone, and the siren's short note sounded, we emerged. A dust cloud covered a pile of rubble that was once home. No one hidden in the other bomb shelter survived. As we left, the sight of dead bodies, asphalt streets in flames, and skeleton structures of bombed-out buildings seared our memory.

With Königsberg destroyed, we moved in with my aunt and uncle, a farmer and mayor of his community. Everyone feared a Russian invasion, and my uncle often met secretly with other farmers. "Line the bottom of a covered wagon with straw. Stockpile canned goods and warm blankets. Keep a fresh team of horses, ready to go at all times," he urged. "I will send out the town crier when the Russians come. Above all, keep quiet about this!" Hitler had issued standing orders to shoot anyone intending to flee.

When the town crier rang his bell late one night, Mama bundled us in layers of underwear, tights, socks, shirts, sweaters, skirts, dresses, gloves, scarves, and hats, and we joined the sea of covered wagons heading west. Prussian farmers feared the Russian army more than Hitler's henchmen, and thus we braved ice, snow, and deadly cold on the trail. When an ear infection led to a high fever, Mama abandoned the wagon train in Danzig, where she found a doctor to treat me.

Every night, the sky grew a brighter orange as we listened to the dull thudding of gunfire from afar. When the Germans destroyed all the surrounding bridges, Mama knew she had to find a way out. When she went to a building near the docks, seeking passage to Denmark, a German officer accosted her. "What are you doing here, woman! You should be digging ditches to defend our great army!"

"Sir, my husband died fighting this war. My three little girls are my only concern now!" Mama explained, speaking softly. "I must lead them to safety."

"I am not concerned with your problems! You know better than to flee! Don't you know I could shoot you on sight? What is your name? Where do you live?"

Mama answered his questions, quaking with fear, but politely, and still he barked, "If you are not out digging ditches by six in the morning, I will shoot you myself. Do you understand?" Mama numbly nodded her head and studied her worn shoes until the brute left. All hope drained, and at last she cried bitterly. A young sailor tapped her shoulder and gazed into her watery, blue eyes, "Ma'am, can I help you?"

Mama shared her story between sobs. "I'm so sorry," he said softly. "You're in the wrong office." He gave her directions and added, "You must hurry."

Mama raced through the building and soon booked a passage on a boat leaving for Denmark at 4 A.M. Again, she quickly gathered our few belongings and ushered us aboard *The Hektor*. The very next night, this same ship sank when struck by a phosphor bomb, killing all the refugees and crew. We barely escaped another brush with death!

Hundreds of thousands of women and children poured into Denmark, also a ravaged country. In Copenhagen, Danish authorities detained all Germans and transported us to an island. Armed guards patrolled our camp, consisting of crude wooden barns surrounded by barbed wire. Twelve families lived in each barn, furnished only with a pot-bellied stove and crude, uncomfortable bunk beds. Wind pierced the unchinked walls, causing us to huddle, shivering beneath straw sacks and paper blankets, in efforts to keep warm at night. We ate gruel at every meal and eagerly sought double portions of our biweekly rations of cod liver oil. When hunger gnawed at me, I would beg Mama for bread.

Again and again she had to say, "Child, there is no bread."

Malnutrition left us vulnerable to illnesses. The Danish doctors ignored us, but nurses came regularly, administered shots, and kept detailed records. Some refugees suspected that they were testing experimental vaccines on us, like lab rats. One morning, my mother and I watched my friend Ulli being buried. As we stood at his graveside, his mother, red-faced and in tears, said, "Mietze, how long will your daughters last?"

The next time the nurses came, Mama wrapped us in paper blankets, laid us in a ditch, and covered us with leaves. We knew from the gravity of her voice that we must listen. "Girls, the nurses are coming with shots. You must hide! If I call you, stay very quiet. Take a nice, long nap. You can come out when I tap you with my hand."

When the nurses arrived with their boxes of shots and records and called our names, we kept silent. One asked Mama to find us, so she shouted, "Gertrude! Ingrid! Monika! Quickly, girls! Come for your medicine!"

We pretended we were hibernating mice and stayed hidden in our nest. Eventually, Mama turned to the nurse and apologized, "The girls must be playing. This is a very big camp." As my mother suspected, when we repeated this game three or four times, the nurses lost interest in us. We survived the next three years in Denmark, shot-free.

When the war was over, few survived with their families intact. My sisters and I survived and live in freedom today because of the unfailing courage and spunk of my mother—my Mietze, my hero.

TAMMY L. GLASER, a 1985 graduate of the United States Naval Academy, lives in Manning, South Carolina, with her husband, Steve. She has homeschooled her two children since 1995. She also writes a blog and manages an e-mail list for families homeschooling children with autism (*www.aut2bhomeincarolina.blogspot.com*). Her mother narrated these childhood memories of her acts of courage in World War II.

There Is No Such Thing as a Perfect Vacuum

CHAVAWN KELLEY

My mother always had an Electrolux—a heavy metal cleaning machine from Sweden with a canister shaped like a bullet. The suction hose was covered in an intricate herringbone of gray and teal, the wand was shiny, and the brush attachment was pure boar bristle. When you were done, you gave the cord a whack, and it flew into a cavity inside the body.

Mother worked all day to keep our house clean. I never thought much of it until one day I went to a friend's house, and her mother was laid out on the couch watching *The Mike Douglas Show*. My mother never did that! My mother dressed in baggy pants and a bleach-stained shirt that had been washed and worn to utter softness. Over her soft mother's bosom, she pinned the lost straight pins she picked up off the floor. She changed sheets once a week, folded towels so the edges didn't show, and kept a jar of soap slivers to melt together for further use. She could cut an apple so the seeds made a star.

My mother was beautiful, and we lived in her world. Summer mornings, draped across sofa, chair, and floor, my sister, brother, and I watched *The Price Is Right*. With the commercials to instruct us, we mastered the vocabulary of domestic deficiency. We chanted disparagements such as "ring around the collar," "tough, greasy heel marks," and "dry, cracked dishpan hands."

At noon, we bellied up to the bar and ordered fried bologna sandwiches. Mother slapped them onto paper plates and with three flicks of her wrist opened a round of Dr Pepper for us. We carried our lunches out the sliding glass door and ate at a green child-sized table on the patio. There, Houston's thick humidity swallowed us whole as we devoured our warm and greasy nurture.

In the afternoons around four, Mother took a shower, changed from her cleaning clothes, put on lipstick—usually orange to match her auburn hair—and started fixing dinner. By the time Daddy drove up, she and the meal both smelled delicious.

My mother was an artist. She majored in art in college, but only one of her pictures ever hung in our house: a watercolor painting of a derelict cotton gin. The inked-in lines of the structure were fluid and sparse and in places, blotched. The colors still looked wet. By staring at that painting, I learned that art is an expression of the soul and need not be pretty to be beautiful.

Mother and Daddy moved to California after they married, and Mother got a job while Daddy finished his business degree. As she tells it, she had two choices: She could ink in the cells of Disney animated features, such as *Cinderella*, or she could work as a technical illustrator for Rocketdyne. She chose the latter. Sometimes in the evenings, she and Daddy drove up into the Hollywood Hills and watched the men she worked for launch fledgling rockets in the cool, minty dusk.

Soon after Daddy graduated, I was born, and Mother quit her job. My baby picture shows me under the Christmas tree beside a Sunbeam mixer. A few years later, we moved to Dallas, and when the Mercury spacecraft passed over our ranch-style house, Mother stood in the driveway with her two little girls and cried. There was no one to tell her story to—how she had made her contribution to the space program in pen and ink.

When we got older, it seemed that on Tuesdays and Thursdays, Mother advised my sister and me to plan for a career. On Mondays and Wednesdays she counseled us to marry well.

I got my first real job at twenty-two, after our family moved to Atlanta. Ellman's was a catalog retailer that sold jewelry, gifts, and household goods, and I was hired as their junior copywriter. The Ellman's motto was "If you don't mind spending less!" And when they hired me, they didn't mind. Even with the 25 percent discount, I couldn't afford a vacuum cleaner—or perhaps I didn't care enough about owning one. Mother gave me a yellow Eureka for Christmas, wrapped up and tied with a bow.

At Ellman's, I learned how to spell *vacuum*, and like thousands of copywriters before me, and maybe a few thousand since, I was overcome by the urge to headline a two-page spread with "Nothing Sucks Like a Hoover."

Some days I lingered over the diamond rings pictured inside the catalog cover. My boyfriend at the time was a pharmacist, smart, energetic, and kind. I sometimes wanted to be a bride, but I wasn't so sure about being a wife. The third time I declined his proposal, he left. Mother might have been more specific about Fridays, Saturdays, and Sundays, the days I needed it most.

I work as a technical editor now, making engineering reports sound articulate for the government. The musician I married in a cottonwood grove wasn't the groom my parents had in mind, but at the moment we became husband and wife, the black veil of the sky dissolved into a shower of spectacular, shimmering light. Who could mistake a sign such as that?

These days, my vacuum is not an Electrolux. It has no shiny parts. It is an upright made of space-age plastics, utilizing dual-cyclone technology and a HEPA (high-efficiency particulate air) filter. I enjoy the eleven amps of power at my control. I've even joined "the Fantom Revolution," according to the video that came with the machine.

When I start the Fantom, my cat Zora awakens, leaving a downy wad of fur wafting as she flies from the room. With my new Fantom, I remove flying fur, hapless hair, and shed skin. I fight fungus and manage mold down to 0.3 microns. I devastate entire colonies of dust mites. But the electrostatic charge of its plastic attracts a Teddy bear coat of fuzz; when I empty the cylinder and a cloud of dust rises into my eyes, I wonder why it has a HEPA filter at all?

Sometimes, when I think of my mother, I imagine one of her primitive rockets launched in the cool of the evening from atop the Hollywood Hills. I almost feel it careening through a distant void, eventually floating toward a few spare molecules. Sometimes I ask my six-year-old son if he'd like me to cut an apple so it makes a star.

CHAVAWN KELLEY likes vacuuming but prefers writing stories. She has received awards and recognition from Creative Nonfiction, Best American Essays, the Wyoming Arts Council, the Ucross Foundation, and the Can Serrat International Art Center (Spain). She lives in Laramie, Wyoming, with her husband and son.

The Storyteller

JOSHUA J. MARK

Ma is smiling down at me from the front porch as I step off the school bus and stomp angrily across the front lawn.

She says, "I guess I don't have to ask how the day went."

I am ten years old, in the third grade and hating every minute of it.

"Come on in," she says, and, her hand on my shoulder, leads me through the front door.

I plop down at the small table in the kitchen, not speaking, still thinking of the school day and how I hate math and how much harder it all seems than second grade was. Ma is getting me a snack out of the refrigerator.

She says, "Hey, have I ever told you the story from the magic book about the creatures that came up from the grass?"

I sigh and, looking up at her, say, "No."

"Well, then," she says. "We'll have to take care of that right now."

She sets a glass of milk and two small, round coffee cakes on a white plate down in front of me and begins, "Once upon a time there was this young boy named Alain who lived in a castle by a huge waterfall. The castle was surrounded by a moat, which was fed by the waterfall, you see, and, with all this water everywhere, the long, green lawns, which sloped down from the castle, were always healthy and beautiful and soft to the touch . . . "

My mother would begin one of her stories, and I would be swept away. It didn't matter if it was a problem at school, a fight with a friend, or an illness, whatever problem I was having would vanish beneath the sound of her voice, and, when reality returned, I'd find myself in a much better frame of mind to deal with whatever I had been upset about. In the tale of the creatures that came up from the grass, for example, Alain discovers that the beautiful lawns that surround the castle are not kept so lush by all the water in the area, but, rather, that the perfect lawns are comprised of creatures called "Shags" that are held prisoner there by a magic spell cast by the new wizard his father just hired. Alain must outsmart the wizard, reveal him to be an evil man who's imprisoning the Shags, and get his father to fire the man. Once freed, the Shags wriggle and flap their way back to their home-land, and the lawns, though no longer perfect looking, are still fine to play ball on.

All of these stories my mother would tell came from a magic book she said she had read years ago and still remembered perfectly. I was often sick as a child, suffering from a problem with my kidneys, and Ma would be the one to drive me to the doctor's offices or the hospital, sit with me through blood tests and exams, and, always, when I was feeling at my lowest, I would hear her voice near me or beside me saying, "Say, have I ever told you the story from the magic book about . . . "

My favorite tale from the magic book was about a young boy named Rohlan. He was always very sick and was frailer and weaker than his younger brother and sister. Like many of the characters inhabiting the stories from the magic book, Rohlan and his family lived in a castle by a large lake. One day an evil sorcerer came and kidnapped Rohlan's brother and sister and scurried across the lake with them to his dark tower. Though sick and in pain, Rohlan mustered the strength to row across the lake by himself, avoid the sea monsters, defeat the sorcerer in a grand duel up and down staircases, and save his siblings.

I loved that story so much I would ask her to tell it again and again. She would always agree to do so, but would say, "Well, before I tell that one would you like to hear the one about the boy at the edge of the cliff?" Who could resist an offer like that? Once she had told the tale of the boy at the edge of the cliff or the flying purple orbs that spat fire, I would be so enrapt with the new tale that I would forget all about my old favorite.

The years passed, and I grew up to be healthy, attend college, and become a writer and a teacher. I stopped by Ma's house one day, when I was in my early twenties, just recently married and starting out on my career, and we sat and had coffee at the small table in the kitchen where she, long ago, would serve me my after school snacks.

We talked for a while about life, and then drifted back to the past. I said, "You know, some of my favorite memories are of this room and you telling me the stories out of the magic book."

Ma smiled and nodded. "Even though they were bad times, I remember them fondly myself. Especially the stories and how much you loved them."

"You know, I don't think you ever did tell me my favorite except for that one time. Actually, do you still have the magic book? I'd like to read it myself now."

Ma laughed and, shaking her head, said, "There never was a magic book."

"What?"

"There never was any magic book. I made all those stories up on the spot."

I couldn't believe what I was hearing.

"Those stories were amazing," I said. "They were the greatest things I'd ever heard. You made them up?"

"I made them up. That's why I could never tell you your favorite one about the boy rowing across the lake. I'd forget how they went as soon as I said 'the end' most of the time."

"Absolutely amazing," I said. I looked around the old kitchen, remembering the past and all my times with Ma. I said to her, "You know, no matter how bad I was feeling, or how sick, your stories always took all the badness away."

"I know," she said, smiling. "That's why I told them to you."

JOSHUA J. MARK is a freelance writer living in upstate New York with his wife, Betsy, and daughter, Emily. Thanks to his mother's inspiration, he pulled the same "magic book" routine on Emily and found that he could not remember his own stories after telling them any better than his mother could. Emily is forever waiting to hear her own "favorite" again.

She Won Her Battle but Never Fired a Gun

RONALD HURST

My mother never won any medals, nor ever fired a gun, but she fought a battle that lasted for much of the forty-eight years she lived. Born in a terraced slum in a decayed industrial area of the English city of Sheffield in 1904, she married the boy next door on Christmas Eve 1927. I was born in 1933, the third of her three sons. My father, wracked with tuberculosis, died when I was two years old.

Legally blind from birth and with three young boys, in those days of high unemployment, my mother could not get work. She walked a couple of miles to the post office each week to pick up her widow's pension of only twenty-one shillings, but it was not enough, and often we went hungry. To stave off malnutrition, the City Council provided a tablespoon of malt a day and a tablespoon of a sickly sweet cordial called Parish's Food.

Each Monday, mother did the washing. After boiling the clothes in a gas-fired copper, she had to pound them clean in her barrel shaped dolly tub. We took turns to wind the handle of the mangle that squeezed out some of the water before she hung the clothes out in our small garden.

On Tuesdays, she baked four loaves in her coal-fired oven. They had to last us all the week. Each week my maternal grandmother baked us a Sally Lunn cake, a highly nutritious breadlike round loaf made with eggs and currants. Each weekday morning, we walked the two miles to Hartley Brook School, to receive a thick slice of bread. They would put jam on it one day, and then drippings on it the next. After eating the bread, we walked back to attend our own school. Still, it was not enough, and I still have deformities caused by rickets, a disease of malnutrition. My mother must have worried, and clearly suffered loneliness and privation, but she never complained. She always remained strong and gave us plenty of love, the only thing she had in abundance.

In 1939, the war brought food rationing. Ironically, we ate better then than we ever did before. Careful planning by the Ministry of Food and strict government regulations meant even the poorest people had a balanced diet at prices they could afford.

We were older, and, with so many men away in the forces, there was plenty of work, even for a legally blind woman with three small boys. My mother found work as a cleaner in a local hospital, where she worked twelve hours a day with one day off in eight, for thirty-five shillings a week. After work, and on her one day off, she had to look after us and do most of the housework. We did our best to help in the house, but we were young boys and full of mischief. In spite of Mother's long working hours, she always seemed to be there when we needed her.

The first night the bombers came, my mother woke us up and led us out to our Anderson shelter, a corrugated iron box sunk to half its depth in the thick clay soil of our garden. Though I was still half-asleep when she snatched me out of bed, I can still remember the sound of the aircraft overhead. It made a throbbing sound utterly unlike any aircraft I had ever heard before. The shelter had a foot of water in it, so mother held us close as we stood shivering in the icy water for an hour before the all-clear signal sounded.

The next day my mother obtained an iron single bedstead and an old mattress from somewhere and placed it in the shelter to keep us above the water level. The mattress soon became moldy, but at least we were damp rather than wet. From then on, the bombers came most nights, so we slept in the shelter all the time—the four of us lying across the bed. My brothers and I were short enough, but how my mother managed to curl up with us, I wouldn't know.

The bombers mostly flew overhead to drop their bombs somewhere else. Antiaircraft guns around us blasted away all night. At five o'clock one morning, after spending all night in the shelter with us, when mother left for her twelve-hour shift at the hospital, she found a piece of shrapnel buried six inches deep in the asphalt of the yard just feet from us.

One night, we heard the scream of a stick of bombs coming very close. They seemed to take forever to fall. Mother hugged us close in her arms, reassuring us and appearing far calmer than she must have felt. One hit a house about fifty yards south of us, and the other buried itself in the roadway fifty yards north. Neither bomb exploded. About two hours later, a third bomb fell even closer and did not explode. The wardens told my mother to keep us in the shelter until they could deal with them. We were frightened, but so exhausted we slept in the damp bed, comforted, as always, by our mother's calm presence.

Early the next morning, our grandfather came to see if we were all right. Armed soldiers ordered him to keep away. He told them to get lost and walked through to us, passing within feet of one of the bombs, and then he conducted us out the same way, tiptoeing until we were past the bomb. Grandfather and Mother showed the same quiet courage by simply holding our hands as if we were not dodging unexploded bombs, but merely on a Sunday stroll.

During the war, because people had to work where the government told them to, Mother had no option but to remain in her arduous cleaning job at the hospital. Once the war ended, Mother could choose where she wanted to work. She always wanted to be a nurse, but being legally blind, she was not permitted to train for that. Instead, she took a job as an orderly in a home for intellectually disabled children, which she enjoyed. After some years, the matron offered to appoint her as a psychiatric nurse, and even though she had to take a pay cut, it fulfilled her lifelong ambition.

My mother worked happily in this field until three months after my twenty-first birthday when she died of breast cancer and overwork. She brought us up with love, kindness, and endless patience until we all reached adulthood. Thanks to her, my brothers and I have led happy, successful lives. I never knew my father, but I'm sure he received her with pride when she rejoined him.

RONALD HURST earned degrees in mathematics, geophysics, and computing. He taught elementary and high school and currently creates animated interactive teaching programs on popular science topics.

Faux Pearls

KIM CAMPBELL

"Hold still." My mother was removing a huge safety pin from her mouth; any wiggling on my part might result in a sudden sharp prick. She tugged the oversized waistband of the black silk skirt tight and slipped the pin into the elastic. "Now . . . can you breathe?" I nodded and tried to ignore the itch on my knee—very hard for a five year old, especially when excited about possibly winning the "Best Halloween Costume" prize in kindergarten. "Remember to pick the skirt up when you walk so you won't trip on the hem."

My mother then turned her attention to my long curly strands. "It's a good thing gypsies have wild hair," she said, tickling the back of my neck. She reached for a bright red scarf lying on her dresser and wove it into my curls. "Gypsy queens like color."

A few days earlier, after reading the note from my kindergarten teacher about the costume contest, Mother had stepped back to look me up and down. "I see a gypsy. Yes, a very pretty gypsy."

I was thrilled she thought I could be a very pretty anything. And if my mother said gypsy would be a good costume, gypsy it would be.

"You need makeup."

Nobody touched my mother's makeup, and if she was going to let me wear her blue eye shadow to school, it was a very big deal. I swished my hips back and forth, listening to the rustle of the skirt.

"Stop that." Mom said, laughing. "I don't want to get any in your eye."

I tried not to blink but couldn't stop giggling. "It feels funny," I said.

A broad grin spread across my mother's beautiful face. "Well remember, you're far too pretty for makeup. Today is just pretend. We're playing dress up."

When she grabbed a tube of lipstick, my heart fluttered. "Lipstick too?"

"No respectable gypsy queen would go without lipstick."

I glanced in the mirror as she painted my lips red. She puffed the crisp golden sleeves of my blouse and smoothed the skirt that seemed to shine when the light hit it just right. Mom then fiddled with the scarf in my hair and opened a small compact. The pink powder she dotted on my cheeks smelled sweet. My nose began to wiggle, and I sneezed.

"Enough makeup," she said, closing the top drawer of her dresser.

I twirled and watched my skirt take flight.

"Now, some pizzazz." Mom retrieved two gold bangles from her jewelry box.

I was so excited my palms began to sweat. Jewelry? She was really going to let me wear her special jewelry? She slid the bangles on my right arm and added a multicolored bracelet on my left, and then added a long strand of black beads and a shorter string of blue. They clacked together as she dropped them over my head.

"What about those?" I pointed at a shiny pearl necklace.

She paused and then snapped the box closed. "Not those. Sorry."

"But they're so pretty. Gypsy queens need pretty things." I suddenly wanted those pearls more than anything.

"Colorful things," she corrected. "I said colorful."

"But, Mommy, please let me wear them, please?"

"Honey, my mother left me those pearls when she died. And even though they're faux pearls, they're special to me. I don't want anything to happen to them."

"Faux pearls?"

"They aren't real." She picked up the hairbrush and fussed with my curls.

I fidgeted, rocking gently back and forth on the heels of my black mary-janes. "I'll be careful, Mommy, really careful . . . promise."

She opened the box and stared at the necklace for several long seconds, and then turned to look into my eyes. She could never deny me anything. "Okay, but you *have* to be careful. No tugging or swinging them around."

I nodded, smiled, and jumped up and down. Their smooth texture proved so seductive I rubbed them between my fingers on the drive to school.

"Don't play with them, or they'll break," she warned.

"Okay," I said, wondering how just touching them could make them break.

Soon after I shoved the car door open and bounded in to meet my classmates. Witches, pirates, Frankenstein, and Cinderella noisily chatted in the room decorated with carved pumpkins, spider webs, and skeletons. My mother had been right. I was the only gypsy. Settling into my desk, I once again fingered the smooth pearls.

"All right, boys and girls, I want you to each stand and show your costumes," Mrs. Hardy said.

Silence fell over the room, but the excitement of eighteen five year olds electrified the air. When my turn came, I was so excited to be a pretty gypsy, as I stood up I gave the pearls around my neck a little swing. The necklace suddenly went slack, and I heard the pearls hitting the tile floor. One little girl beside me let out a gasp, and the rest of the children fell to their knees to gather the bouncing bobbles.

Tears filled my eyes. Mom had known exactly what would happen if I wore the pearls, and it didn't matter whether they were real or not. They had been a gift from her mother. I had ruined something that could not be replaced.

Mrs. Hardy put the pearls in an envelope for me to take home. I didn't win the "Best Costume" prize, but in my mind, I no longer deserved it. The only thing I could think about was how disappointed my mother's face would look when I confessed that I had done exactly what she told me not to do.

When the afternoon bell rang, sounding louder than usual, I trudged outside. Mother smiled and waved from the car. A lump formed in my throat and tears ran down my cheeks as I reached for the door handle.

"What's the matter?" she asked as I fell into the seat. "Oh, you didn't win, poor darling, but you're still a very pretty gypsy.

"I-I broke it," I said, my hand shaking as I handed her the envelope. "I'm so sorry, Mommy."

My beautiful mother stared at the envelope for several minutes and then smiled wanly. "It's all right, Kim."

"Really?"

"Not entirely," she said, reaching to gently wipe tears from my cheek. "But I know you didn't mean to break them, and they're just faux pearls after all." When she slid the envelope into her purse, I noticed a slight quiver in her chin, but she never mentioned the pearls again—ever.

KIM CAMPBELL, a native Texan, is a freelance writer, editor, and business owner. She has published many articles and short stories in major magazines and enjoys helping writers find their own paths to publication. Married to the love of her life, Kim lives down the street from her parents and stills spends many precious occasions with her mother.

Bombshells

DOMINICK CALSOLARO JR.

It all started a week before my robotics team planned to go to Hartford for the regional competition. The trip was going to last four days, which meant four whole days and three nights alone with my friends—having fun. At last I was going to have a break from the nightly arguments at home. I didn't have many opportunities to get away from my family's craziness, nor from my annoying Mom, so when this competition offered me a respite, I was pumped.

I had been looking forward to the trip for a month when Mom dropped a bombshell. "Since I've worked so much overtime in the past few months, I have enough vacation time to go to Hartford with your team!" And the thing is, she looked incredibly happy and expected me to be happy. I was not happy. My main reason for going on the trip had evaporated in a flash.

Sure I would still enjoy the competition, and my friends. But I had envisioned the trip as an escape, and now I would have to spend four days and three nights with my mom constantly looking over my shoulder and interfering with everything my friends and I wanted to do. Mom had a way of embarrassing me in front of everyone.

The week leading up to the competition, Mom and I bickered constantly. I tried every angle I could think of to talk her out of going on the trip, but it always ended in a huge argument that my stubborn Mom won. She wouldn't change her mind no matter what I said. At first I tried to be nice to her, saying that she wouldn't know anyone, and that she probably had better things to do with her time. When that failed, I reminded her that she would be the *only* parent going from our team, but she didn't even blink. Finally, I went with the big guns. I told her how I felt. I came right out and said that she would embarrass me, and that the real reason I wanted to go on the trip was to get away from her, not to spend more time with her. As you might imagine, that didn't go over too well, and a chilly impasse created a void that carried over to the competition.

On the bus ride to Connecticut, I avoided my mom as best I could by acting like I didn't notice her. When we arrived in Hartford, I dodged her as much as possible. When she got up to go somewhere, I glued myself to the bleachers; when she came back, I got up and found something else to do. When we returned to the hotel at night, I scurried off to my room with my friends and didn't think twice about what she might be doing. When Mom signed on to chaperone at the pool, I stayed behind with a few of my friends, even though I really wanted to swim with the rest of my team members. Every night at dinner, I sat as far away from her as possible and found ingenious ways to completely ignore her.

Despite all of my efforts, she still managed to embarrass me. At the competition she cheered like a maniac, focusing everyone's attention on her instead of the current match. If she happened to walk over to my friends and me when we were doing something we weren't supposed to do—like watching a movie during a match—she forced us stop whatever we were doing (even if we weren't bothering anyone) and insisted we join the rest of the team. But nothing she did throughout the competition compared to what she did during the closing ceremony.

Woody, one of the popular cofounders of the competition, was the guest speaker and when they introduced him, the crowd went wild, my mom along with everyone else. During his speech, however, everyone else sat quietly, listening intently—all except one person. My mom. Whenever Woody said something she agreed with, Mom yelled—at the top of her voice—"We love you Woody!" Occasionally, she screamed—at the top of her lungs. Every single person in that convention center could hear her. I buried my face in embarrassment, alternately praying that no one knew she was my mom and that Woody's seemingly endless speech would come to an abrupt end. I felt mortified and vowed to never speak to my mom again—ever.

Meanwhile the leader of our team had decided not to stay for the award ceremonies and suddenly signaled for the team to follow him to our bus. Completely out of control, Mom had edged closer to the stage to snap a picture of Woody. When she didn't show up, I realized that Mom might actually miss the bus. For some reason, this unnerved me. I decided to put aside my feelings and ran back to find her.

I had to search for five minutes before I found her gabbing to people on the far side of the convention center. "Mom, the team is leaving," I said, rolling my eyes. Mom just looked at me like *I* was being dramatic. We barely made it back in time to board the bus before it left the center.

When we arrived home, I still acted tense, like she was a pain, but she made a big deal out of the fact I had come looking for her, and I (for some illogical reason) suddenly realized that in that moment I felt grateful that she was my mother. It baffled me, really, until I finally figured out that this must be love. Love is more than just a feeling. Sometimes it's an invisible bond that forms between people. And maybe the strongest bond of all is not one that forms between two atoms, or anything like that. The strongest bond just may be the one that exists between a child and a mother.

DOMINICK CALSOLARO JR. attends Albany High School in Albany, New York, and looks forward to going away to college and majoring in computer science. He plays on the varsity soccer team, participates in both the robotics club and the chess club, and manages to make the principal's list every quarter.

The Art of Graceful Dining

SUSAN REYNOLDS

Grace Sue Pennington grew up on a small tobacco farm in Paris, Tennessee, in the shadow of war. When she met a handsome discharged sailor ten years her senior, at an ice skating rink in the summer of 1944, and a whirlwind romance ensued, they married quickly and moved to Georgia. A mother by nineteen—and soon thereafter the mother of five—she never had time to achieve sophistication. In fact, her life became one of constant struggle. Regardless of their meager circumstances, my mother remained a southern lady who wore pleated skirt dresses, high heels, bright red lipstick, and demure pearls. She may not have ended up with the life she wanted, but she decided early on to properly acculturate her children.

Stunningly beautiful with thick, wavy black hair—always brushed backward to highlight her strong face—brown eyes, a wide flawless smile, alabaster skin, and a tall, slender, shapely form, my mother exuded the elegance of Jackie Kennedy paired with the presence of Ava Gardner. In the proper setting, she could easily have been what she liked to call "*swellegant.*" Alas, her husband's war wounds left him emotionally and physically challenged. While my father tried, he also frequently fell apart and disappeared repeatedly for "long rests" that I didn't learn until much later were stays in psychiatric wards. My staunchly *southern lady* mother held the family together, consistently putting meals on the table while both guiding and disciplining five children.

When my father's business went bankrupt, and he migrated north to work on a huge power plant, my mother managed all five children and a part-time job. A year later, my mother packed up the entire household and drove the family's Packard, pulling a trailer, from Albany, Georgia, north to Pittsburgh. When their eldest, sixteen-year-old daughter was diagnosed with a malignant brain tumor, underwent a radical operation that resulted in paralysis of the entire left side of her body and a child-like mental capacity, my mother cared for her day and night for more than two years. When my father disappeared into the hospital for a year, leaving us to survive on welfare, my mother kept a smile on her face and grit in her back pocket. She sewed clothes for her three girls, mended her sons' clothing, glued together our shoes, and shushed us when we complained. And when her eldest daughter died, my proud mother dealt with it all—alone—without revealing to anyone, not even her parents, how dire things became.

No one would have blamed her if she had weakened or "thrown in the towel," as she bemoaned often about others. Luckily, my mother had a steely resolve and coped by remaining the quintessential *southern lady*—focused on manners, propriety, and charm. "Don't slouch, Susan," she'd admonish often. "Elbows off the table, skirts down over the knees, legs together, backs up straight, heads held high, never speak with your mouth full, and no chewing gum—ever!"

At the dinner table, we were schooled in the art of being polite. "Social discourse," my mother would say, "requires intelligence, eloquence, and manners." To her, dinnertime was sacrosanct— the forum for decorum. She taught us to delicately place napkins on our laps, chew with our mouths closed, sit up straight, avoid laughter or shouting, and conduct polite conversation.

Meals began and ended with manners. After prayers, the fried chicken and mashed potatoes made their circuit, each dish being offered to the person on your left, and then passing each to your right. No one began eating until all were served. Small portions were replenished by graciously requests: "Please pass the potatoes" or "May I have some more butter, please?" My mother taught us to always say "thank you," and to always remain seated and attentive, unless we absolutely required an excuse to leave the table, at which point, we always asked, "May I please be excused?"

She also had strict rules for how a proper young woman dressed. In junior high, when the popular girls wore mini-skirts and pantyhose, my mother insisted I wear knee-length skirts and knee socks to school. Even though most girls wore bell bottoms or frayed denim shorts to all casual events, my southern mother expected her daughters to wear skirts and dresses—even to the local summer carnival! If I dared to come downstairs in jeans, she would leap from her chair. "You are not leaving the house dressed like that, young lady. Go right up to your room and change."

Rebellious and headstrong, I battled what I saw as my mother's outdated conservatism and often spent my weekends grounded. Safely away at college, I gleefully breached her rules. I wore ridiculously short mini-skirts and ragged bell-bottoms everywhere (but church), burned my bra and shredded my girdles, disagreed with my professors, talked out of turn, and even shouted slogans at anti-war demonstrations—all things my mother would have never done. I turned my back on my mother's ways of thinking and acting, rejecting her in the process.

However, when I landed a job at a publishing company in New York City and was soon hobnobbing with bigwig fashion designers, I suddenly embraced everything my mother taught me. The unsophisticated farm girl from Tennessee had given me the armature I needed to dress for success, speak intelligently, act like a lady, and always know how to behave in even the most elegant social setting. When I found myself seated at a table with a coterie of French designers, I not only donned an inexpensive, yet ladylike dress—accessorized with a simple string of fake pearls and tasteful black pumps—I was able to politely request the salt, inquire about their latest presidential election, and mention the sudden drop in the hemlines as a possible reflection of a social backlash. Thanks to my mother's lessons in the graceful art of dining, I moved in a larger world and became a better woman because of it.

Twenty years later, when sorting through my mother's boxes of memorabilia, I came across a scrapbook from her high school days. There, in her neat, perfectly formed cursive handwriting, I found ten pages on social and dining etiquette, including "proper" place-setting arrangements, details on which fork was used for which course, a listing of the three most elegant china and silver manufacturers, directions on how to formally serve tea, and descriptions of which shape wine glass best accommodated particular wines.

Sadly, my beautiful mother never had the life she deserved. She never owned china or silver, never dined with French designers, never brushed elbows at a Hollywood cocktail party with the likes of Cary Grant and Elizabeth Taylor, and never pursued a career in New York City—but she spent many long years making sure her children could damn well do so if they pleased. My mother has been gone ten years, but whenever I feel the need, I retrieve her scrapbook and delicately smooth the edges of her tattered list, relishing the one place the *swellegance* of Grace Sue Pennington still breathes.

SUSAN REYNOLDS is a freelance editor and author. She authored *Change Your Shoes, Change Your Life*, as well as three other nonfiction books and is currently editing Adams Media's *Hero* series. Happily, she followed in her mother's footsteps and taught her two children, Brooke and Brett Aved, the art of graceful dining, as well as many other useful social graces. Learn more about Susan, and upcoming anthologies, at *www .literarycottage.com.*

Tap Dancing with Grandma

BEVERLY HALEY HADDEN

By the time Grandma and I reach the corner of north Denver's West 38th and Tennyson, my shoes can barely contain my tapping toes. Tall letters over the white portal entry announce "Elitch Gardens."

We step into the shade of the ticket window. Grandma squeezes my hand, and then snaps open her pocketbook. She counts out the coins knotted in her handkerchief and pushes the exact change through the half-circle cutout in the glass window. I try not to stare at the lady's mountain of blonde curls, her pencil-thin arch of eyebrows.

"One adult and one child, please," Grandma says. She's acting proper, but inside she's as tingly and giggly as I am. We've been counting coins and days till the time we could watch the school kids take tap dancing lessons.

The towering attendant in his crisp blue uniform feeds our tickets to the steel receptacle's trap door, and then bows as he ushers us through the turnstile. We enter a marvelous world of thick-leafed trees and fat snowball bushes lining a winding path through the sculpted gardens. Grandma inhales the fragrance of the flowers. But my eight-year-old patience wears thin.

"Hurry, Grandma," I coax, tugging the skirt of her familiar blue cotton dress with white polka dots.

"No rush," she says and smiles. "We mustn't miss anything along the way."

"But the Trocadero's so far . . . " I wail, but stop when she raises a finger to her lips.

Beyond the wide lawns of flowerbeds, small children straddle carousel ponies. Dare devil passengers cling white-fisted to their seats when the Wildcat dives straight down, then grinds steeply up.

I tug at Grandma's skirt. Soon the path leads up alongside the theatre. The ancient wood structure stands like a noble aristocrat, strangely silent, waiting for night to light its marquee, fling wide its doors, and fill its seats with chattering playgoers. Grandma points to the rows of black-and-white photos of Hollywood stars, all of who have acted here—Clark Gable, Claudette Colbert, Walter Pidgeon.

"Come on, Grandma," I say. "We can't miss the tap dancing."

Her mouth turns up in an impish grin. She quickens her pace.

Skipping ahead, I whirl back, skip ahead, whirl back, and skip ahead again. The sounds of music grow louder till we're face to face with the Trocadero dance pavilion. Daytime is for kids' tap dancing; but night is for live orchestras and grownups' ballroom. I'd been told my parents danced here during their college days, but I couldn't capture that picture. Besides, this was now. This was Grandma and I.

One wall of the pavilion is rolled up. I stare, rude or not, at the slender man seated at the piano. His fingers fly over the keys, both feet pump the pedals. Children wearing black patent shoes tied with wide grosgrain bows click to the beat (well, almost all). The floor's shining surface mirrors their images.

Suddenly shy now that we're here, I hang back.

"Come on," Grandma says, mimicking me, and marches us to the front row of empty seats. "Watch closely," she says. "Memorize the moves."

She leans forward from her slender waist, her sun-freckled hands resting on the chair's arms. I remember how those hands, softer than rose petals, washed mine in a bowl of warm soapsuds when I was little.

Sweeping my eyes around the ballroom makes me think of Grandma's cedar chest where dance prizes, lying tissue-wrapped among other treasures, tell enchanted stories from her youth. Though I couldn't picture my parents as young, I can clearly see a thick auburn-haired version of my grandmother in a swirling white gown, floating on the arm of a smiling, handsome fellow— the pair, wrapped in the joy of the dance, ignoring the stiff-faced judges scowling over their scored cards.

I blink and the long ago scene vanishes. I focus on the row of children on the dance floor, study their feet and movements. "Shuffle left, turn, bow," the teacher directs.

The younger children make way for an older group dancing complicated patterns—so much to see, and to remember. Too soon the pianist's hands are still, the children clickety-clack off the floor. The Trocadero echoes with sudden silence.

Grandma and I sigh, push the seats (screeching) up, and find a private picnic place beneath a maple tree. We spread a freshly pressed patterned flour sack over the wooden table, dense with carved initials of past picnickers. Grandma anchors the cloth with our brown bag lunch.

"Now," she says, hands on hips, feet planted on the concrete, "time for the test."

"Oh," I say, glaring at our shoes. "If only we had shiny black tap shoes."

"Pshaw," Grandma says, "just let the magic happen."

Her shoes shuffle, the heel of her right shoe taps smartly, and Grandma whirls and curtsies. "Was it that way?"

"Ummmm . . . this way, I think." I try the steps.

"That's it! You've got it. Let's do it together from the beginning."

I pretend I'm the girl at the end of the line, the one with bouncy, golden Shirley Temple curls. My hair is brown and bobbed; Grandma's hair is gray and bobbed.

Congratulating ourselves, we sink down at the table, hungry for lunch.

"There, now, who says we're not every bit as good as they are?" Grandma's blue eyes twinkle at me. She hands me a sandwich and an apple.

I take a bite of peanut butter and raspberry jam (Grandma's and my favorite.), pause, and look at her.

"Is it stealing to spy on the lessons?"

She brushes my question away. "No law against watching. So what if we learn from it, too?"

Still, I roll the faint taste of stolen pleasure on my tongue. The last crumb of our picnic disappears. Grandma folds the paper bag and tucks it into her pocketbook.

We half hop, half skip along the tree-lined sidewalk back to Grandma's house. On a slab of cement near the back porch, we dance the tap pattern again. Two beady-eyed squirrels in the weeping willow stoop chasing one another's tails to stare. We giggle.

* * *

Years ago a wrecking crew leveled the Trocadero. Not so long ago the old Gardens were abandoned in favor of a glittering high-tech amusement park downtown.

Grandma, too, is gone. In my heart's eye I see her smiling and tap dancing through the great white portal of the Garden of Forever.

When my turn comes, she'll meet me there, take my hand, and we'll dance to our hearts' content. Perhaps a pair of beady-eyed squirrels in a weeping willow tree will stop chasing one another's tails to stare.

BEVERLY HALEY HADDEN writes from her home in Fort Collins, Colorado. Her first writings were letters scribbled to the grandmother in this story, and she's been writing ever since, particularly personal essays, reminiscences, poetry, and fiction for kids.

Celestial Moos

JAN HENRIKSON

"Are you inflammable again, my dear?" Mom asked at the precise moment gas leaked from the hose onto my shoes. She sat in the passenger seat of my getaway car, blinking her blue-lidded eyes, waiting for me to get us on the road again.

Yes, I was combustible. I'd just wrenched myself from a seven-year marriage with a perfectly nice corporate man in Chicago so I could launch a new life with a free-spirited writer in Florida. All my belongings sat in twisted white trash bags in the back of my Honda.

Even scarier—I was about to spend 3,000 miles alone in my car with my sixty-six-year-old mother.

Don't get me wrong. I liked my mother, but she was Queen of *Better Safe Than Sorry*. For thirty years, she'd longed to dye her hair. Unfortunately, as a youth she had misread the warnings on a Clairol box and feared she'd end up blind instead of blonde. Years later she grabbed another box on impulse and experienced a shock of clarity: The warnings were for eyebrows only. She laughed and lightened right up.

As I paid for the gas, I watched her watching me from the car window in her wide-brimmed straw hat with the red sash, and I saw fear. After all, she'd made my sisters and me wear daisy-decaled rubber swim caps as we splashed around the *wading pool* in our driveway. After dinner, she demanded we sit on our back porch for a half-hour before playing, to prevent cramps. She once mistook the scent of Love's Baby Soft cologne on my T-shirt for a popular recreational drug.

I'd always held Mom close to my heart but closed, like a fan, never beholding the lively design hidden in the folds. I didn't realize that for much of my childhood she was weakened from a rare blood disease; I didn't appreciate the gift of her sitting in that tiny pool with us, donning her own swim cap. (If she couldn't protect her health, at least she could protect ours.) And, although her nose misled her when I was a teen, two years later, when I really was in trouble with drugs, she never gave up on me.

Never mind all that. On this reality-shaking ride, I insisted I was the brave one, an explorer voyaging onward into an unknown world—with my mother sitting next to me, making sure I arrived safely.

Arriving safely could prove tricky; neither of us knew how to read a map. We'd spent hours of our lives, separately and together, on wild rides in strange parts of even stranger towns. Still, yellow-highlighted maps in hand, we persisted. For backup, my dad recorded travel tapes, the predecessor of the GPS system: "Up ahead three miles is the exit for I-89 A—don't take it!" or "See the turnoff for a two-lane road by a Denny's at mile marker 219? Bypass it!"

We nibbled on milk chocolate Hershey's bars with almonds, and Dad's famous fudge before breakfast, after breakfast, at every rest stop. We flew down the freeways to Florida, in ever-increasing heat, our tanless Illinois thighs sticking to vinyl.

I kept waiting for a 3,000-mile interrogation: "How could you leave your home, your husband, your dog? What do you know about this guy Michael, anyway?" Followed by tears and more advice.

But all I got was laughter. Not once did she question my decision. I was so ridiculously in love with my new love that I plastered his photos on the dashboard: one of him brushing his teeth, another of him leaning against the wall of a fast food restaurant wearing a shirt with a huge stain over his heart.

By the time we cruised into Chattanooga, Mom and my soul mate were hitting it off. "Hi, Michael," she'd say whimsically, leaning toward the photo. "How do you like the ride? Are you comfy? Are we driving too fast?"

Who was this woman? "Take a picture of me," she demanded playfully at a restaurant one night. "I'm a photojournalist at large. You may have my autograph." Indeed, she was a photojournalist at large, embarking on her next career at an age when most people retired. I'd witnessed her on the job two days before we left. In her black knit dress, black beret, and jade necklace, she cut quite a dashing figure. People fell under the spell of her eyes and before they knew it, their life stories flew out.

Mom folded her arms on the table and grinned as I snapped the picture. "I'm going to send you a life-sized cutout of me for your new apartment," she teased. "You can stand it in the living room."

I began to realize that for nearly thirty years, I'd misread my mother's label. She'd let me evolve while I'd frozen her into some distorted old image. How much courage she'd had to raise three daughters, to go back to work at age fifty, to face a life-threatening illness by buying red shoes as a symbol of life.

She wasn't spacey, as I once suspected. A shrewd comedienne, she just liked to play. For years, she'd been gently putting the whole family on. Now she was downright slaphappy. By the time we crossed the state line to the Florida Promised Land, she was communicating with the local fauna.

"Moo!" She leaned her head out the car window and called to all the cows, which looked strangely out of place under palm trees.

At that moment, I didn't just love her for her mean moo. But for her shimmering presence, her offbeat way of showering acceptance on me and herself and life's unpredictable detours.

She'd done that all along, hadn't she? "That's life, kid," she sometimes said with a shrug about abrupt life changes. When I'd called her earlier to tell her my marriage was over and there was something else she should know, she chirped, "Are you in love with a woman? It's okay. You can tell me anything. I watch Oprah Winfrey."

At last I'd opened my mother's fan—and my whole being expanded.

We stepped out of the car, chocolate-stained and goofy with pride. Not once did we get lost on this trip. It's never happened again.

But that's life, kid.

JAN HENRIKSON writes, edits, and thanks her lucky stars for such a whimsical mother. Her essays have appeared in *A Cup of Comfort®️ for Writers, Chicken Soup for the Dieter's Soul,* and *Simple Pleasures of Friendship,* among other publications. She is editor of *Eat by Choice, Not by Habit* (Puddle Dancer Press, 2005) by Sylvia Haskvitz.

Facing the Night

BARBARA GILSTRAP

In 1951, years before anyone talked about female empowerment, we lived in the country five miles outside a small town in Texas. My father worked away from home during the week, and sometimes for weeks at a time, leaving Mama and me manless, carless, telephoneless, and scared to death.

A lot of Highway 64 traffic zoomed past our house, and Mama was convinced that most of it consisted of criminals looking for their next victims. She would lie awake night after night listening for cars to slow down and stop.

Her fear was no doubt enflamed by the *True Detective* magazines she regularly bought and read cover to cover. These rags told true stories about girls and women—always "good people" who did not deserve it—being stalked and murdered in gruesome ways. Mama forbade me to read them, but of course I did when she wasn't watching me.

Our fear was further stoked by a weekly radio show called *Inner Sanctum*, which we never missed. It began each week with the terrifying sound of a slowly opening, creaking door and the diabolical voice of the host: "Good evening, friends. Enter a gay little world of homicidal maniacs, vampires, ghosts, were-wolves." I would hang onto Mama's dress tail the whole time the program aired.

I also hung onto her dress tail while she went through her nightly ritual of what she called "deburglarizing." When night began to fall and she had locked all the doors, she would go through the entire house, shining the flashlight ahead of her as she jerked open closet doors and combed the dark space under the beds with her light. Once she even borrowed my cousin's dog to follow her through the house as she tried to ferret out culprits.

I was too scared to sleep alone, so Mama let me sleep with her when my father wasn't there. One night she woke me up in the wee hours by leaping out of bed. I asked her what was wrong as I tried to pull myself from sleep.

"Sssh," she whispered. "I hear something."

Without turning on a light, she began to make a silent sweep of the house. Meanwhile, I was entirely too scared to stay there without her, so I slipped out of bed and began to crawl on the floor toward where I thought she was. Because we were both moving stealthily to elude the "assailant," I didn't hear her coming, and she didn't know I was there until she had stepped on my hand. When she felt warm flesh under her bare foot, she let out a throat-splitting scream a millisecond before I shrieked at the top of my eight-year-old lungs. After we realized what had happened and that we were all right, we held each other and cried. Then, when it dawned on us that our screaming had not roused any neighbors, we knew that whatever might happen to us in the future, no one would ever come to our aid.

Our nearest neighbors were Mr. Jake and Miz Minnie, who were in their sixties. Mr. Jake ran a small country store that sold groceries, gasoline, and all the daily necessities. He liked to live well and indulged himself in whatever he wanted, whether it was allowed or not—candy and Coca-Colas, despite his diabetes, and stolen kisses from our neighbor Miz Lula, despite the fact they were both married to other people.

Fortunately for us, he liked to go to the picture show, and he invited a few of the neighbors to go with him and Miz Minnie to see *Show Boat*. He and Miz Minnie sat in the cab of his pickup, along with Miz Lula. Mama and I rode in the back of the pickup with Tommy and Nan, a teen-aged brother and sister who were as thrilled as we were about this excursion. A refreshing summer breeze whipped our hair as we sped through the night under a star-filled sky to see the gods and goddesses of our time.

Afterward we were all smitten with the movie, and especially with Ava Gardner, whom we had not seen before. Miz Lula remarked that Mama looked a lot like Ava, and everyone else agreed. Mama protested, but I could tell she was pleased.

Our bliss was short-lived. Before the week was out, our long-dreaded prowler had appeared. Just after we had finished our baths and were getting ready for bed, Mama heard rustling in the honeysuckle vines outside our bedroom window. She immediately turned out the light and shushed me. She was awake all that night listening, and the next morning she found footprints in the flowerbed outside the window.

A few nights later it happened again. This time Mama shined her flashlight through the window and shouted, "I know you're there." Whoever it was didn't stir until we finally went to bed and lay there breathing shallowly.

Then it happened one more time. By now Mama was too riled up to cower. She ran to the back door, flung it open, and held her flashlight on the fleeing figure. Her hands trembled as she locked the back door and turned to me. "What in the world will I do?" she said quietly. "It's Mr. Jake."

I was only a child, but I knew she could not report Mr. Jake to the sheriff. We owed him a lot of money for our groceries, and he'd cut off our credit at the store. She took turns being scared and angry as she walked the floor. Finally she made me go to bed while she stayed up worrying. By morning, she had come up with a solution.

It was a pearl-handled pistol, which her brother got for her and showed her how to load. I begged her not to shoot it, as I imagined my own mother in the pages of *True Detective*, not as a victim, but as a murderer.

"Don't worry," she said, as she set up a line of tin cans in our backyard. "You stand way back now." I did, because I always had a good sense of danger.

She didn't even come close to the cans with the first few shots, but her aim improved as she practiced. When she finally hit one, she began to whistle.

"What's going on?" Mr. Jake demanded, as if he had the right to know. He was standing at the edge of our yard.

Mama glanced at him before she gave a deadeye aim and struck another tin can. The pinging sound rang through the air.

"I've had a peeping Tom lately," she replied. "I'm going to be ready for him the next time he shows up." Then she creased another can.

Mr. Jake turned around and walked back into his store without saying another word.

That fall Mama got a job digging sweet potatoes for a local farmer and paid off our grocery bill at Mr. Jake's store. Our prowler never returned, and Mama never again lay awake at night.

BARBARA GILSTRAP has written plays, screenplays, and a young-adult novel, *Smart Girl*. One of her plays, *The Alto Part*, was produced in New York and is published by Samuel French. Her screenplay *Gotham Guide* was a quarter finalist in the Nicholl Screenwriting Competition.

Blue Circle Books

ALISON MILLER BONIFACE

My mother marched through the front entrance and up the stairs, heading for the second floor of the school. Down the hall she strode, tall and purposeful as her shiny cap of brown hair bobbed above the plaid collar of her coat. My six-year-old legs could barely keep up.

"Mom, wait," I pleaded, half out of breath. *They're just circles*, I wanted to say. *It doesn't matter. I can wait until next year.* Suddenly this seemed like a bad idea. I wished I had kept my mouth shut.

But it was too late for second-guessing. My mother wasn't about to slow down, not to glance at the bulletin board outside my classroom, and not to respond when my first-grade teacher, dressed in the cheery red suit I loved, who waved from the doorway and proffered her wide "Parents' Night" smile.

"We'll be right there," my mother said." We have an important meeting in the library first." "Mom," I tugged on her sleeve, trying to curb her momentum, "It's okay . . . really." I hadn't intended to make such a big deal about it. I liked our school librarian. Mrs. Jacobsen was pretty and dressed nicely and read us stories in a singsong voice that made the stories come to life. No one could make better character voices than she. What if my mom made her so mad that she banned me from the library? What if she said I couldn't take out any books at all? The horror of it chilled me straight through.

We turned the corner and stopped outside the library door. Inside the glass display case stood the covers to all my favorites: *Make Way for Ducklings, Curious George, The Lorax.* I sighed. There was no stopping my mother now. When she set her mind to something, no one could sway her.

Dressed for the special occasion in her frilly white blouse and tweed skirt, Mrs. Jacobsen sat pertly at the desk. "Hello, I'm Marilyn Miller," my mother said, and then reached down to take my hand. "Alison's mother."

"Of course," Mrs. Jacobsen said, removing her half-glasses and smiling down at me. "Alison's a wonderful reader for her age."

I puffed up at the compliment. With a December birthday, I'd be turning seven in a couple of weeks, long before most of my first grade classmates.

"Yes, she is." My mother paused, and her hazel eyes flashed. "But last week, she told her father and me something that bothered us."

"Oh?" Mrs. Jacobsen frowned, my mother bristled, and I studied the carpet beneath my feet.

"She said something about not being able to take out 'blue circle books.'"

My gaze lifted. Scattered around the library, attached to shelves at varying heights, hung red and blue circles made from construction paper. Like stop and go lights, they directed us where we could go—and where we couldn't.

"Well, yes," Mrs. Jacobsen answered slowly. "First-graders may take out any book from the shelves marked with red circles. The blue circle shelves are for the older students, in second and third grade. Those books are more difficult reading, and a little too challenging for the younger ones." She beamed at me. "We don't want the children to become discouraged, just as they're learning to read."

My mother straightened her back. "Alison has been reading since she was three."

I stared at my mother, surprised at the certain, proud tone in her voice. "Her father and I would very much prefer that she be allowed to make her own choices about which books to borrow."

My gaze moved from the lift in my mother's chin and the calm strength in her eyes, to the librarian's face, which had paled ever so slightly.

A long silence ensued, before Mrs. Jacobsen folded. "Of course. I didn't mean . . ."

"And if she wants to borrow more than one book at a time, we'd like her to be able to do that too."

That was the other rule, the one I hated: only one red circle book at a time. I could read one of those baby books in less than ten minutes! What did Mrs. Jacobsen expect me to do with the rest of my weekend?

Mrs. Jacobsen, looking flustered and slightly perturbed, fiddled with her glasses. My mother stood her ground. "Well . . . ah . . . if you feel that strongly about it, I'm sure we can make an exception."

Tension flowed out of the room, and my mother flashed her warmest smile for the first time since we'd arrived at the school. "Thank you, Mrs. Jacobsen."

No longer afraid of imagined consequences and feeling jubilant, I patted my hands together in a silent clap. My mother had triumphed. I could read books from the blue circle shelves. I could take out more than one book at a time! I felt so giddy at the prospect, when my mother turned and strode down the hall to see my first grade teacher, I snuck back to the N-O-P section. I'd had my eye on the new *Amelia Bedelia* book for a couple of weeks. When I walked past the books with their baby stories and silly pictures on the red circle shelves, I felt so grown up I tingled. I snatched the desired book off the shelf, checked it out, and ran to catch up with my mother.

Later that evening, my father asked in a low voice, "Did you get our little problem taken care of, Marilyn?" My mother nodded. And though my head bobbed in sleep my six-year old heart swelled. That was what mothers did. They took care of problems. When you had rights but were too small or too cowardly to face them, they stepped in. They took on your scary situations and let other people know exactly how smart you were. They believed in you, and in doing so, they taught you to believe in yourself.

By the end of that school year, I had read every blue circle book in the library.

ALISON MILLER BONIFACE is a high school English teacher and published author of women's fiction and contemporary romance novels. She lives with her husband in the northern New York City suburbs. Her love of language and of reading dates back to the day her marvelous mother stood up to the school librarian. View her work at *www.allieboniface.com*.

Tu Sei Bella

PATRICIA LJUTIC

We sat on the front porch, an island my grandmother rarely ventured beyond, and where I chose to sit beside her. Blinded when she was twelve by an Italian folk remedy meant to heal an eye infection, Grandma could see only light and shadow, and she knew me more through touch than sight. She sat on a lawn chair and I on the cast iron bench, so close our thighs touched. She cupped my forearm in her hand. Her touch was warm and soft. When she stroked my arm, it felt as if she was inviting me to melt into her. I rested my head against her shoulder, and even the slight scent of her perspiration seemed sweet, like oranges. She never pushed me away, and the melody of her voice soothed me.

We seldom had time together. She lived in New Jersey, and my family lived a hundred miles away in New York, a distance far enough that my parents made the trip only twice a year: for Easter and during the summer. When we visited Grandma, I longed to find time alone with her, but our gatherings were an occasion for my aunts, uncles, and cousins to assemble for large Italian feasts that started with a breakfast of pastries, biscotti, eggs, onions, and potatoes, and went on all day long, straight through antipasto, bread, meat pies, ham, meatballs, lasagna, and rolled flank steak. I observed Grandma as she rolled herbs between her fingers and smelled them, placed her fingers into bowls or cups to feel the level of the liquids, and tasted the sauces. The men watched sports on television and listened to Neapolitan folk songs and Dean Martin. The women helped cook and wash the dishes, set the table, and chatted about the weight they never lost. While the conversations, cooking, and consuming went on, I played baseball, Simon says and hide-and-seek with my sister and cousins, waiting for the calm when I could have my moments with Grandma.

At home I had given up. From a very young age, I was told by my parents that they were miserable being my mom and dad, and that they only kept me because they had to. "This is not your house!" my father roared at me at least twice a week. "It belongs to your mother and me. You're here because we let you be here."

My mother didn't defend me. I tried to stay out of her way by hiding under the end tables, playing quietly on my bed, or finding a place in the field behind our house. No matter what I did, something about it irritated her.

"I'm just waiting until you turn eighteen," she'd hiss at me. "Then you can be on your own, and I won't be responsible for you anymore. It's a thankless job being a parent, thankless."

Daily, one or both of my parents said something deliberately unkind to me. I was called stupid, lazy, ridiculous, hysterical, a burden, ungrateful, and useless. Positive or tender exchanges were rare. Acceptance and affection depended upon conditions I could never meet. I could not be sweet enough, obedient enough, or tidy enough. I could not tuck the bed sheets in tight enough, or comb my frizzy hair straight enough. I could not read well enough, move fast enough, or dry the drinking glasses without leaving water spots. My father ranted that my walking through the living room had worn a path in their wall-to-wall carpet, and that carpets cost money. My eczema and my shoes cost money. Couldn't I wear those shoes a little longer? I couldn't.

I felt frozen stiff. I tried to comply, and to not be a bother or burden to my parents. I longed to be accepted and worthy of their love. Whenever I tried to adapt and become whom they said they wanted, I failed.

Grandma understood, even if only intuitively. Her mother died giving birth to her, and soon after, her father immigrated to the United States, leaving Grandma with his mother in Italy. Over the years, Grandma moved from household to household, making herself useful: cooking, cleaning, caring for children, and harvesting grapes. She never said how being blinded affected her, nor complained, but she did tell me that she helped stomp grapes for wine, and that she never told anyone what went on in the homes where she stayed.

"If I did," she said, "they'd kick me out."

Eventually, her father finally brought her to the United States to care for the four children he had with his second wife. Even there, she didn't have a secure home. Her stepmother resented her and complained about her constantly. Grandma once admitted that she married my grandfather to escape her father's house. Perhaps Grandma saw in me the homelessness she had suffered.

My grandmother, Vincenza, offered me sanctuary. When I stayed with her, I'd open the refrigerator and find a glass of cold grapefruit and orange juice she had mixed for me. I'd wake up to her pulling up the shades on the bedroom windows while singing, "You Are My Sunshine, My Only Sunshine." In the middle of the day, Grandma would take out her tambourine and sing, while my sister and I danced the tarantella. It didn't matter that we didn't know the steps. When Grandma told us it was a tarantula's dance, and told us to go a little wild, we did our best to gyrate like a couple of huge, hopping spiders. She taught us how to balance wide, fleshy leaves on the thumb-end of our fists, blow into them and pop them, making a soft, organic *poof* sound. Placing her thumb firmly under her loose upper-teeth, she made them wiggle and made fun of herself. We spent hours laughing together, until our sides hurt.

Grandma Vincenza was my adult. At home, what love I experienced was always coupled with anger and resentment. At Grandma's, love was unconditional, laced with acceptance and joy. Because of her, I knew that not everyone threatened to throw children out into the street for being useless; that as a mom, I could open my heart and home to my children and give them everything I had, and in return receive more love than I ever anticipated possible.

On those hot humid days when we sat together, the only two people in the world, Grandma welcomed me to rest against her, while she rubbed my arm.

"Tu sei bella," she said. I knew what it meant without her telling me: "*You are beautiful.*"

It meant everything.

PATRICIA LJUTIC lives with her family in Pinole, California. Her poetry, articles, memoir, and humorous essays address spiritual and maternal themes. Her work has appeared in the *Contra Costa Times*, *Circle Magazine*, and *Marin Writes*. She named her daughter Vincenza and loves telling her how much she loves her and singing "You Are My Sunshine" in memory of the Grandma who taught her about love.

Stories My Mother Told Me

PAUL ALAN FAHEY

"Honey, did I ever tell you about meeting Steinbeck at a party in Salinas? I spoke of my mice, he of his men."

* * *

"I'm thinking of Butcher's," Mother said, as she put the 1949 Hudson in gear, checked her makeup in the rearview mirror, and told me to sit back in my seat. Knowing Mother was off and running, literally, I settled down and gave her my full attention.

"We lived thirteen blocks away at the time and had to do all our shopping at Butcher's. Simply no other grocery stores nearby, Honey. We could have gotten into our cars, I guess, driven to a neighboring town, but during the Depression, we really had no choice. The cost of gas was an arm and a leg."

During my 1950s childhood, Mother often told me stories, reflections on her youth she viewed as a retreat to a happier period in her life. Sometimes she spoke about the family home at 413 Hazel in San Bruno, and at others, about her girlhood escapades. In the 1930s, Mother rode a trolley to St. Paul's, a private, Catholic high school, but she often skipped classes with her girlfriends. They'd stay on the car all the way into town, to the Market Street terminal. Then, after eating a waffle dripping with butter and syrup at Bunny's Coffee Shop, they'd sneak into the balcony at the St. Francis Theater and sip whiskey and smoke while Bette Davis urged Paul Henreid not to ask for the moon, they already had the stars.

> *"Whenever I came into the shop," Mother continued, "Mrs. Butcher would yell back to the help, 'don't worry about Mary Eileen. She knows what she's looking for. Drag out one of my kitchen chairs, Abe. She can't reach the canned goods without it.' And oh, the penny candy, Honey. Why did it always look so great in Lent?"*

Mother told me stories mostly to entertain and take the edge off my nomadic childhood. We were gypsies then, a mother and son, drifting up and down the San Francisco Peninsula, shifting addresses and staying one step ahead of creditors and outraged landlords. Monday night might be a motel room with kitchenette and a free continental breakfast then Wednesday, a furnished studio apartment. I never knew where we'd end up. Week after week, month after month, we dragged around our cardboard suitcases, a box of family photographs, and a set of copper-bottomed cookware from San Mateo to Palo Alto, cheerfully ignoring those pink, third warning utility bills that piled up in our mailboxes.

Years later, in a failed attempt to organize the household garage, I came across a carton marked, "Mom's Memorabilia." I cut through the yellow-edged packing tape, and underneath a copy of *St. Paul's Tattletale*—its final issue dedicated to the Blessed Virgin, Mary our Mother and Queen—I discovered a program from Edgemont Elementary. My mother, Mary Eileen Smith, had played an assistant clerk in the eighth-grade pageant titled, "Naturalization, the Making of a Citizen." My mother. Who knew? This was definitely a story I'd never heard.

I flipped through a handwritten composition on the Crusades, with the letters, JMJ, an acronym for Jesus, Mary, and Joseph, topping each page. Then came a religion test on the sacrament of matrimony with a blank space after the question, "What is meant by the banns of marriage?" I read Sister's comment, "Don't you know this, Mary Eileen," and I had to laugh. Separated twice from my father, divorced, and remarried later in life, Mother had little to say about the sanctity of marriage vows. Even then.

> *"Where was I, honey? Oh, yes, Butcher's. The penny candy, and atop the glass counter sat the punch board."*
> *"Punch board?" I asked. "You mean a punch bowl."*

"No, no. no. A rectangular board with numbered holes and bits of paper rolled up inside. Like a checkerboard, I guess. You paid the clerk a penny, punched out a number and won a prize. You might get a jawbreaker, an Abba Zabba, or even a Three Musketeers. I can still taste the vanilla, strawberry and chocolate flavors. Those were the days, Honey.

One time, Esther and I were browsing at Butcher's and discovered there were only twelve chances left on the board. We didn't have the money, and it was Good Friday to boot. We ran the thirteen blocks home, cajoled our mother into giving us the money, then flew back to the store, bought the remaining chances and returned home. Unfortunately we couldn't do much more than admire our treasures and yearn, at least not until after Easter Sunday Mass. Your Grandma was a stickler and didn't allow no candy eatin' in Lent."

Before closing the binder, I skimmed the inside back cover and read the farewell notes from Mother's high school classmates. I imagined I could hear their adolescent voices, some soft, almost musical, others louder with a South City drawl:

To a swell gal.
To Mary Eileen, the society belle,
what she'll do next one never can tell.
To somebody who is liked and loved by all.
To the little country girl from San Bruno.

I returned the denim binder to the box and carefully placed the other items inside before securing the cardboard flaps with strips of heavy-duty tape. The task wasn't difficult because the art of packing had become second nature to me, a useful talent I'd mastered years ago, along with the ability to focus on the present and let the future take care of itself. *Living for the moment*, Mother called this.

But that's another story.

PAUL ALAN FAHEY was the editor of *Mindprints, A Literary Journal*, a national forum for writers and artists with disabilities. His fiction is currently online at *Crimson Highway*, the *Boston Review*, and in the print issues of the *Loyalhanna Review* and *Skive Magazine*. Paul's mother, Mary Eileen (Smith) Nugent was a great friend and mentor who kept him feeling safe and secure in an unconventional and rather uncertain childhood.